MVFOL

ideals®
CHRISTMAS

More Than 50 Years of Celebrating Life's Most Treasured Moments

Vol. 57, No. 6

Shall we not to the whole world say—
God bless you! It is Christmas Day!
—*Georgia Douglas Johnson*

IDEALS—Vol. 57, No. 6 November MM IDEALS (ISSN 0019-137X)
is published six times a year: January, March, May, July, September, and November by
IDEALS PUBLICATIONS, a division of Guideposts
535 Metroplex Drive, Suite 250, Nashville, TN 37211.
Periodicals postage paid at Nashville, Tennessee, and additional mailing offices.
Copyright © MM by IDEALS PUBLICATIONS, a division of Guideposts
POSTMASTER: Send address changes to Ideals, PO Box 305300,
Nashville, TN 37230. All rights reserved.

Title IDEALS registered U.S. Patent Office.
SINGLE ISSUE—U.S. $5.95 USD; Higher in Canada
ONE-YEAR SUBSCRIPTION—U.S. $19.95 USD; Canada $36.00 CDN (incl. GST and shipping); Foreign $29.95 USD
TWO-YEAR SUBSCRIPTION—U.S. $35.95 USD; Canada $66.50 CDN (incl. GST and shipping); Foreign $55.95 USD

The paper used in this publication meets the minimum requirements of
American National Standard for Information Sciences—
Permanence of Paper for Printed Library Materials, ANSI Z39.48-1984.

Subscribers may call customer service at 1-800-558-4343 to make address changes.
Unsolicited manuscripts will not be returned without a self-addressed, stamped envelope.

ISBN 0-8249-1164-4 GST 893989236

Visit *Ideals*'s website at www.idealspublications.com

D0506546

Cover
Boughs of Holly
Multnomah County, Oregon
Photo by Steve Terrill

Inside Front Cover
CHRISTMAS EVE
Walter Anderson, Artist
Fine Art Photographic
Library Ltd.

Inside Back Cover
BRINGING IN THE CHRISTMAS TREE
P. Grim, Artist
Superstock

A Winter Eden

Robert Frost

A winter garden in an alder swamp,
Where conies now come out to sun and romp,
As near a paradise as it can be
And not melt snow or start a dormant tree.

It lifts existence on a plane of snow
One level higher than the earth below,
One level nearer heaven overhead,
And last year's berries shining scarlet red.

It lifts a gaunt luxuriating beast
Where he can stretch and hold his highest feast
On some wild apple tree's young, tender bark,
What well may prove the year's high girdle mark.

So near to paradise all pairing ends:
Here loveless birds now flock as winter friends,
Content with bud-inspecting. They presume
To say which buds are leaf and which are bloom.

A feather-hammer gives a double knock.
This Eden day is done at two o'clock.
An hour of winter day might seem too short
To make it worth life's while to wake and sport.

Transformation

Sudie Stuart Hager

My summer garden was my pride.
When winter came with blustering stride,
My heart went sick at havoc wrought
On pool and lilies, poppy beds,
Soft rose-cups, dahlias' stately heads,
Fringed asters, golden mums—all bought
With months of sun-toil. Then one morning
My eyes went wide at night's adorning—
The pool a fluted, crystal bowl,
The asters gay in starched lace frocks,
Tulle bridal trains on hollyhocks,
Each poppy bed a tinselled knoll.
My summer garden was a treasure,
But lovely this, exceeding measure!

Winter Garden

Sudie Stuart Hager

What can a winter garden grow
With frost-numbed earth, a crust of snow,
And sleet-filled winds that lash and freeze?
Alabaster ferns and grass,
Flowers of opalescent glass,
And pearl-branched, silver-fruited trees!

A garden is blanketed in snow in VIEW TO GAZEBO, AFTERNOON IN WINTER,
CERNEY HOUSE *by British artist Charles Neal. Image by Superstock.*

ICE CASCADES
Brian F. King

Now rock and rill where tricklets flowed
Are fused into a wondrous sight,
Where winter-captured waters glow
With sun by day, with stars by night.
Like blue-white tresses, streams are held
Suspended in the frigid air,
Since icy winds their waters stilled
And left them locked in splendor there.

Gray walls of stone with glory draped
Are radiant in their robes of ice.
Small birdlings pause the sight to see,
To chirp and trill, "How nice! How nice!"
Oh, there is nowhere in the world
A loveliness of which to sing
Than where the touch of winter's hand
Has captured rivulets of spring.

ICEBOUND
Mary E. Linton

And now the ice-bound river knows restraint.
The sea must wait,
While frozen in the veins of earth the pulse is lost.
My song that flows from some eternal spring
Must learn of winter now,
Must know the grip of ice, the glacier's pace.
But answering the same high call,
My heart will hold its faith till spring,
Knowing well all rivers reach at last the waiting sea.

Oregon's Silver Falls breaks through the winter ice.
Photo by Dennis Frates/Oregon Scenics.

WINTER SUNSHINE

Patience Strong

Sun in winter thrills us more than June's bright golden blaze.
Sun in winter, lighting up the drear and dismal days,
Shedding its transforming power benignly, secretly,
Waking into sudden life the stark and leafless tree.

Sun in winter, breaking through a rift among the clouds.
Sun in winter, shining on the faces of the crowds
Like a smile, beneficent, upon the world's old face,
Changing to a loveliness the drab and commonplace.

So Love's touch upon a heart that has grown cold with fear;
In its warm enfolding glow, doubts melt and disappear.
Searching out the frozen places with its magic ray,
Just like winter sunshine on a cold and dreary day.

A SUNNY ROOM IN WINTER

Grace Noll Crowell

Summer is captured here, the warmth and light
Of fire and sun send out their golden glow.
A bright canary trills its keen delight
In liquid notes that leap and splash and flow;
And from a bulb bowl piercing fronds arise,
A miniature green forest, pebble-strewn.
There is mid-summer in the light that lies
Across the rug this winter afternoon.

And such a sense of peace and deep content
Pervades this old worn room—such sunny cheer.
So many orderly and safe days are spent
Within its walls—such happiness is here.
So comfortable the chairs beside the hearth;
I love it more than any place on earth.

Left: The warmth and light of summer is captured in this sunny room in winter. Photo by Jessie Walker Associates.
Overleaf: The crimson walls of Clinton Mill add Christmas color to the snow-covered New Jersey landscape. Photo by Gene Ahrens.

THROUGH MY WINDOW

Pamela Kennedy

Art by Russ Flint

A Holiday Journey

I was so excited about the holiday season! Our two sons would be joining us in Hawaii, and it would be the first time in two years when everyone would be together for Christmas. I spent the pre-holiday weeks baking favorite cookies, shopping for special gifts, and anticipating lots of time together with the children.

We greeted the boys at the airport with traditional, fragrant flower leis, then laughed and chattered all the way home, in an attempt to catch up on everything in just a few minutes. Unlike the snail-paced days of anticipation, the days now seemed to fly. Too soon it was December twenty-fourth, and their visit was half over! The special times I had dreamed and prayed about hadn't materialized. Our younger son was back into the social scene with friends home from college and spent his time at the beach or at their houses. Our older son seemed preoccupied with upgrading our computer, and he and his sister spent long hours conferring over the latest software applications. It was not what I had anticipated. I wanted to bond, to share, to reestablish relationships.

On the morning of Christmas Eve, our twenty-one-year-old suggested we take a hike together. The mountain range behind our home consisted of steep hillsides and deep valleys. There was a trail, he said, that would lead us to the top of the highest ridge from which we could enjoy a sweeping view of both sides of the island of Oahu.

"It's not a difficult hike. You could do it, Mom," he urged with a smile. The gauntlet was thrown, and I snatched it up. Maybe we could catch up on things as we hiked. We slathered ourselves with sunscreen, filled plastic bottles with water, and headed off to conquer the Koolaus. My husband opted to stay home, not wanting, he explained, to intrude on my "bonding time" with the children.

We started off in high spirits, joking and laughing, teasing one another about who would be the first to complain about the trek. The trail was well marked and began on a gentle incline, winding between pungent eucalyptus and swaying ironwood trees. Hundreds of birds darted through the branches, calling noisily to one another. It was a beautiful morning, breezy and warm. After about twenty minutes, we reached the top of the first ridge and descended into a valley; then the trail took a sharp upward turn, and we began climbing. Due to recent rains, the ground was damp under a carpet of fallen leaves and ironwood needles. This made footing a challenge, and a few times I had to catch myself by grabbing branches along the trail. As the trail grew steeper, the climb became more challenging, and our conversation lagged. Even the youngsters were puffing and panting. I was determined to keep up and be a good sport. After all, who knew when I'd be able to have them all together again? I was third in line, with my older son bringing up the rear. "In case," he said, "Mom needs any help." He isn't particularly athletic, so we all suspected his motives might be just a bit mixed; but as it turned out, he would have ample opportunity to prove the truth of his intentions. After two hours on the trail, we still couldn't see the top of the ridge; and I was beginning to question the wisdom of the whole adventure.

"It can't be much longer," sang out my younger son, the hiking expert. "We've come so far already!" I groaned, took a swig of water, and resolutely planted my foot on a rock in the trail. Loosened by the softened earth, the rock tumbled away and bounced over the side of a ledge into the valley a hundred feet below us. Slipping to my knees, I took off in a slow slide in the same direction. Frantically, I grasped at vines and twigs, but nothing held.

"Josh!" I yelled, "Catch me!" He positioned himself between me and the drop off and lunged toward me as I came sliding by. He grabbed my arm, and we tumbled into a strategically placed tree trunk covered with dirt and dead foliage.

"Mom, that was awesome!" shouted my daughter from her vantage point about fifty feet up the trail. "You should be more careful, you could've gotten hurt! Come on, Doug says the ridge isn't too much farther!" She turned and trekked after her brother.

When my heart slowed, Josh and I disentangled, scraping off the biggest clumps of mud and leaves before rejoining the others. About an hour later we stood on a grassy ridge completely awed by the vista before us. We could see the ocean on both sides of the island. Turquoise melted into deepest indigo. At our feet the mountainsides fell away in shades of green while the tradewinds caressed us with the scent of wildflowers. The four of us grinned at each other. We were dirty and sweaty, but we had made it to the top of the mountain. We sat there for a while, talking about how beautiful it was, how we could hear the birds and insects and the wind brushing the tree branches. It was a communion of sorts, a celebration of past and present, love and family. I looked at the faces of my children, now grown, and thanked God for the blessing each one brought into my life—and for this precious time together.

The Christmas Eve hike was a communion of sorts, a celebration of past and present, love and family.

As we wound our way down the mountainside, I recalled another family and their Advent trek. We would celebrate their journey tonight in a candlelit sanctuary filled with hymns, giving thanks for the gift of their Child. But this afternoon, God had answered my Christmas prayers, in a sanctuary of His making, illuminated by the sun, filled with the songs of birds, and I was overflowing with gratitude for the gift of my own children.

Pamela Kennedy is a freelance writer of short stories, articles, essays, and children's books. Wife of a retired naval officer and mother of three children, she has made her home on both U.S. coasts and currently resides in Honolulu, Hawaii.

Winter Vacancies

Isla Paschal Richardson

When autumn winds have stripped the trees
Of leaves, I do not find it sad.
It is most interesting to learn
About the neighbors I have had.

Though every time I leave the house
I pass a small crepe myrtle tree,
There quite serene, I learned today,
A redbird raised a family.

And from the maple by my door
I've often heard sweet music swelling,
And now the secret is disclosed:
It was a robin's happy dwelling.

And here and there with quick surprise
I find where mother birds have hovered,
Leaving behind their summer homes,
Until today, quite undiscovered.

Winter Signs

Glenn Ward Dresbach

Under the tents of cedar trees
Are feathery tracks of chickadees.
The blue jays stop their scolding now
In splendor from a shaken bough.
We look up through the brief designs
That fall in whispers from the pines.
Below are life's small signatures
On this hushed beauty that endures.
And with the winter signs, we show
Upon this unspoiled page of snow
How surely in it we confide
With our own footsteps, side by side.

A Cardinal in the Snow

Violette Newton

It isn't often that we see the snow.
Our seasons move from green to gold to brown
And back to green, in cycles we all know.
But ah, today there's white upon the ground;
And ah, today my window-watching's paid
Me double-fold: a cardinal has come
To where the feeding grain is newly laid;

And he alights, and he is having some.
I watch him as he moves and dips to eat,
This regal fellow in his scarlet red.
He tracks the snowcrust with his little feet.
He quickly stills, and cocks his crested head.
And in an instant, he is fled away;
But I, I see him all the brilliant day.

A male cardinal braves a Missouri snowfall. Photo by Gay Bumgarner.

WINTER

Bliss Carman

When the winter comes along the river line
And earth has put away her green attire,
With all the pomp of her autumnal pride,
The world is made a sanctuary old,
Where Gothic trees uphold the arch of gray,
And gaunt stone fences on the ridge's crest
Stand like carved screens before a crimson shrine,
Showing the sunset glory through the chinks.
There, like a nun with frosty breath, the soul,
Uplift in adoration, sees the world
Transfigured to a temple of her Lord;
While down the soft blue-shadowed aisles of snow
Night, like a sacristan with silent step,
Passes to light the tapers of the stars.

A path is left through the snow-gowned pines in WOODED
WINTER LANDSCAPE, MORTARATSCH *by artist Peter Mondsted.*
Christie's Images, London/Superstock.

SENTINELS

Avis Turner French

I saw them standing on the hill,
The pine trees decorated by
New fallen snow, the clouds rose-tipped
Within the twilight sky.

I waited patiently to see
The cloud ships sail away; then far
Within the vast immensity,
I saw the evening star.

Somehow it seemed a message came
From lonely pines and star above,
"All clouds will pass but these endure,
Deep beauty, truth, and love."

I saw them standing on the hill,
Each pine a sentinel apart
For quiet things, star grace and snow
And faith within the heart.

Country CHRONICLE
Lansing Christman

AFTER THE SNOW

The storm is clearing." What music those words hold after a December snow. How interesting it is to watch the breakup of the clouds overhead as they part to reveal the expanse of the sky and the sun gleaming down upon the snow.

I find a happiness in the change as I feel the warmth of the winter sun and watch it lighten the blue skies of December. I think of the skies as opening the curtains and shades, opening the very windows of the universe to reveal a transformed earth. The hills lie covered by a deep blanket of white, as though nature had pulled up the covers to shield the earth from the cold.

There was poetry in the rhythm of the falling snowflakes, covering field and pasture and lawn, hiding old stone walls and covering hedges, rooftops, and bird boxes. I watched it clothe the boughs of the evergreens in pristine white. Now I watch the bright red of the cardinals shine against the snow as they move from bough to bough, filling the landscape with music and poetry.

The author of three books, Lansing Christman has contributed to Ideals *for almost thirty years. Mr. Christman has also been published in several American, foreign, and braille anthologies. He lives in rural South Carolina.*

In North Carolina, a wagon waits for spring to come to the Blue Ridge Mountains. Photo by Norman Poole.

SNOWMAN SNIFFLES

N. M. Bodecker

At winter's end a snowman grows
a snowdrop on his carrot nose,

a little, sad late-season sniff
dried by the spring wind's handkerchief.

But day and night the sniffles drop
like flower buds—they never stop,

until you wake and find one day
the cold, old man has run away,

and winter's winds that blow and pass
left drifts of snowdrops in the grass,

reminding us: where such things grow
a snowman sniffed not long ago.

*A young pup seems a bit unsure of his new carrot-nosed friend
in* MY LITTLE SNOWMAN *by artist Donald Zolan. Image copyright
© Zolan Fine Arts, Ltd., Hershey, Pennsylvania.*

A Christmas Prayer

Author Unknown

Give us the faith of innocent children that we may look forward with hope in our hearts to the dawn of happy tomorrows. Reawaken the thought that our most cherished desires will be realized, the things closest to our hearts—that we may come to an appreciation of the limitless joys and bountiful rewards of patience, charity, and sacrifice.

Above all, endow us with the spirit of courage that we may face the perplexities of a troubled world without flinching, imbued with the child-like faith which envisions the beautiful and inspiring things of life. And restore the happy hours and experiences so many of us foolishly believe are lost forever. Give us faith in ourselves and faith in our fellowman. Then the treasures and beauties of life that make humans happy will spring from an inexhaustible source.

And at Christmas, when the hearts of the world swell in joyous celebration, let us cast aside all pretense and live, if only for a day, in the hope and joy we knew as children.

Could every timeworn heart
but see Thee once again,
A happy human child
among the homes of men,
The age of doubt would pass;
the vision of Thy face
Would silently restore
the childhood of the race.
—HENRY VAN DYKE

Artist Albert Chevallier Tayler (1862–1925) captures holiday memories being formed in his painting entitled THE CHRISTMAS TREE. Image from Fine Art Photographic Library Ltd.

A STAR AND SNICKERDOODLES

Aileen Mallory

The bus slowed, then stopped. After several tries at revving up the motor, the driver called out, "Sorry, folks, looks like we're stuck here for a while."

"But tomorrow is Christmas Eve!" came the loud protests from throughout the bus.

"Okay, folks, settle down. I called into town, and we're first on the list for the snowplow."

What next? Sarah thought with a sigh. It was bad enough that she couldn't be home for Christmas. After much resistance, she had reluctantly agreed to visit her daughter, Amy, and her family in Anndale. Sarah blinked back tears as she watched the snowflakes slither down the bus window. Dusk started to settle over the landscape.

There had been so many changes in her life, but until this year at least one tradition had remained. Even after her husband had died, her daughters, Amy and Marilyn, had brought their families to Sarah's home, the family home, for Christmas.

But this year Amy had persisted, "All that work is just too much for you, Mother. Marilyn says she and her kids want to have Christmas in their own home, and Steve thinks we should do the same." Sarah knew her family only wanted the best for her, so finally she gave in. Now here she was, with strangers, stranded in a snowstorm.

"I wanna go home," wailed a four-year-old across the aisle.

"Shhhh, we'll go pretty soon," her mother soothed. "We'll soon see Daddy."

How tired that young mother looks, Sarah thought. She's probably Amy's age.

"Do you have much farther to go?" Sarah asked.

"No, we're getting off at Anndale."

Responding to Sarah's kindness, the young woman was soon sharing her story. Her name was Janice Selby, and she and her young daughters were going to Anndale for Christmas. They would be moving there, but her husband had to go on ahead the week before. His new job at the plant wouldn't wait.

"My boss wouldn't give me my full pay if I didn't finish out the year," Janice explained.

"What are your names?" Sarah asked the girls.

"Becky," said the little one.

Before her sister could answer, Becky added, "Her name's Tiffany. We have a dog, but he's with the neighbors. His name is Popeye." Tiffany explained that the black circle around one eye gave the dog his name.

Becky asked Sarah, "Do you have any kids?"

The older woman and the two little girls settled down to talk. Janice smiled, relieved that somebody else was keeping the girls occupied for a while. Sarah was telling about her grandchildren—Matthew and Susan, their ages and their pets—when the driver's voice came through the speaker's static.

"Listen up, folks. There's been a change of plans." It grew completely quiet on the bus. "The snowplow had an emergency call, and it's headed east of town."

"That's ridiculous!" stormed the bearded man seated behind Sarah. "You said we were first."

Others joined in with "That's right! What happened?"

"Now wait a minute," the driver protested. "This wasn't my idea."

"I'm Martin Fagan, and I have an important business appointment tomorrow. Now just what do you intend to do to get us on our way?"

The reply dripped with sarcasm. "Well, par-don me, Mister Fagan. Some things have priority, you know. There's a stranded bus with a passenger who's due to have a baby any minute. They've got to get that woman to the hospital." After a few low murmurs, people quieted down. Time dragged on, and some passengers slept.

I am tired, Sarah admitted to herself. I probably shouldn't have stayed up so late last night baking cookies. She leaned back, eased off her shoes, and closed her eyes. She roused at Becky's "I'm hungry."

As Sarah opened a box, the sweet, telltale smell of homemade cookies filled the air.

Tiffany asked, "What kind are they?"

"Snickerdoodle," Sarah responded.

Becky burst out laughing. "Snickerdoodle? What's that?"

Her mother explained. "I guess the girls have never heard of snickerdoodle cookies. With a full-time job, I don't do much baking."

Sarah didn't have to ask twice for someone to pass out the cookies. The girls went down the aisle with a frequent "Snickerdoodle cookie anyone?" Then they'd fall into gales of giggles.

There's something about little girls' giggles, Sarah thought. They're contagious. Sure enough, soon everybody was smiling as they munched on cookies and talked with their neighbors.

Even Mr. Fagan grinned as Becky handed him a cookie. He went to the front of the bus and whispered to the driver. What now? Is there a problem? Sarah wondered but then didn't ask. She didn't want to alarm anybody.

Suddenly the bus was plunged into darkness. "Don't panic, folks. I turned off the lights so we won't run down the battery," the driver explained. "I have a flashlight if anybody needs it."

To distract Becky from her impatient complaints, Sarah asked, "Were you in any Christmas programs this year, Becky?"

It seemed that both girls had given recitations at church the previous night. "How would the two of you like to perform a program for us?" Sarah asked.

Becky jumped to her feet. "God is love, the Bible says, and it is true we know. He sent Jesus as a baby, on Christmas long ago."

As people clapped, Becky made a deep bow then said, "Your turn."

Tiffany hesitated. "I need a star. We had one at church, with lights on it." Suddenly she came up with the solution. "I know, a flashlight!"

How could the driver refuse? Tiffany pointed the flashlight to the top of the bus. Her hair shone in the reflected light from the metal ceiling.

"See? Just like the star of Bethlehem," Tiffany said. In the flashlight's glow, she told the age-old story of Jesus' birth and the star over the stable.

There was a moment of complete silence, then applause. Janice started singing "Silent Night." Soon others joined in, carol after carol. There were some off-key and forgotten words, but nobody cared. A deep baritone prevailed, and Sarah noticed it came from Mr. Fagan.

"What a beautiful voice you have," she offered.

"Well, yeah, maybe." Then he admitted, "I sang in the church choir . . . but that was a long time ago."

One by one the voices dwindled away, and soon the bus was quiet once more.

"Okay, folks, the snowplow is on its way," the driver called out.

"And the baby? What about the woman with the baby?" several passengers wanted to know.

"They made it to the hospital just in time. It was a girl." The crowd cheered for a woman they didn't even know and the birth of her child.

Mr. Fagan led off with "Joy to the World." The passengers were still singing when the bus arrived at the station.

"Hey, you guys, thanks for being good sports," the driver said amid the shouts of goodbye and merry Christmas. "Don't rush off. There are special treats for you and your families in the bus station."

Sarah smiled. That explained Mr. Fagan's whispered conversation with the driver earlier. Apparently there had been a candy order relayed to town.

As she followed Janice and the girls down the steps, Sarah saw a tall man in a plaid windbreaker rush toward them. He folded his family into his arms.

Becky looked back over her shoulder as she walked away with her daddy. "Goodbye, Mrs. Snickerdoodle," she shouted.

Then Sarah spotted her own family and hugged her grandchildren as they ran to greet her. Amy helped her mother into the car and said, "Wasn't that a perfectly horrible experience for you, Mom?"

"Well, no, not really. We had our own Christmas celebration with cookies and carols and a star of Bethlehem. There was even a newborn baby."

As they drove away, Sarah gazed out at the moonlight sparkling on the newly fallen snow. A newborn baby—just like the night Jesus came into the world. As clear as if they had been spoken, the words came to her, "For God so loved the world, that He gave His only begotten Son."

Sarah knew that more than Christmas plans might be changing for her in the years ahead—but some things never change.

The design of the cross-stitched "Joyous Advent Calendar" is adapted from the original art by Judith Ann Griffith. Reproduced under license with Inter Art ® Licensing. The design is provided by © DIMENSIONS ®, 1801 N. 12th Street, Reading, PA 19604.

ADVENT CALENDAR

Michelle Prater Burke

As a child, it seemed to require days and days of persistent begging to convince my parents that Thanksgiving was long past and it was time to carry the holiday boxes down from the attic. When they finally relented, we would first flip through the record collection to find the Nat King Cole and Perry Como Christmas albums; then we would initiate the unpacking of the decorations by placing the Nativity scene on the mantel. Mom would bring in the bowl of nuts with the silver nutcracker, and we could crack open a few bites between hanging grade-school Christmas tree ornaments and porcelain tree angels. By the fifth or sixth time Nat

King Cole had crooned about chestnuts roasting on an open fire, our living room had been transformed into the magical place we had awaited all year.

After I grew up and left home for a living room and Christmas tree of my own, many of my childhood holiday traditions seemed misplaced or no longer possible. The first home my husband and I lived in didn't even have a mantel, much less a nutcracker; and our first Christmas tree, though memorable, was adorned after only one carefully budgeted trip to the department store and was much heavier on the fir than the finery. Most of our holiday traditions remained in our parents' homes. After all, that was where we still spent Christmas morning, surrounded by memory makers such as my brother's sequined ornament made in the fourth grade and the felt stocking my mother made for me before I was born.

After the births of my own children, I began thinking about Christmas from the viewpoint of a mother and wondering what sounds and sights of Christmas my children would remember decades from today. What would they tell their children were the best parts of the holidays at home? I decided to begin forming some seasonal traditions that would be unique to our family, and I thought an Advent calendar was the perfect place to start. After all, Advent calendars heighten the anticipation of Christmas and are a wonderful way for the family to count down the weeks of Advent together.

Traditionally, the four weeks leading up to Christmas have been a time of reflection and preparation for the greatest of Christian festivals. Various forms of Advent "calendars" have been used for years to count down the days. In German-speaking countries, Advent wreaths are still quite common and often hold four candles, one lit on each of the four Sundays before Christmas Day. On the last Sunday, all four candles are ceremoniously lit and allowed to burn down. German children are also given Advent candles marked with twenty-four divisions to burn each day until Christmas Eve.

Today, most Advent calendars have evolved from candles to safer options: beginning with the first day of December, a marker on a decorative calendar is moved or an ornament or treat is removed to mark the approaching holiday. The calendars are often made of cloth and needlework, such as feltwork, cross-stitch, or needlepoint. Some calendars are made of heavy board and have numbered windows that open to reveal treats or ornaments. Others are wooden with tiny painted ornaments. Recently I have learned of a modern version of the Advent calendar as well. It is a framed board holding twenty-four tiny wrapped packages. Each festive parcel can be opened to reveal a sweet; the following year the boxes can be refilled and retied to begin the countdown.

To begin my project, I first chose what kind of Advent calendar to make. I was looking for an elegant, traditionally finished product that would fit in well with my other Christmas decorations. Such a calendar could help my family look forward to each new day of the season, culminating in Christmas Day. And by creating the calendar myself, I could make it unique to our family.

Since I had several months in which to complete my calendar project and wanted something colorful, I chose to take on the challenge of a needlework Advent calendar. I found many sorts of kits available in crafts stores. One included patterns for creating twenty-four fabric characters, such as stars or toys, to place each day on a tree-shaped wall hanging. Another had places to tie twenty-four peppermints to be snipped off one by one. I decided upon an elegant cross-stitched pattern that depicts a Christmas quotation and woodland scene; it counts down the days by moving a small brass heart along a row of numbers. The cross-stitch pattern is quite intricate, integrating beadwork and specialty stitches; but I feel it will give the finished product instant heirloom status—exactly what I was looking for. I plan to add personal additions too by stitching my own children's initials next to the small children in the scene.

I hope my children have gleeful memories of unpacking the Advent calendar and beginning the countdown through the days of December.

I hope to have my Advent calendar finished by late November, in time to hang it on the wall and christen an evening of holiday decorating. In the years to come, I plan to reserve a special time of day, such as right after family breakfast or just before bedtime, to gather the children and move the calendar's heart one day closer to Christmas. After all, a family is a mixture of past, present, and future; and by spending the holidays enjoying established traditions and creating new ones, we are building our future together. Some day when my grown children think of their Christmases past, I hope they have gleeful memories of unpacking the Advent calendar and beginning the countdown through the days of December while the voice of Nat King Cole in the background joyously welcomes the season.

SKATING

Herbert Asquith

When I try to skate,
My feet are so wary
They grit and they grate;
And then I watch Mary
Easily gliding
Like an ice-fairy,
Skimming and curving,
Out and in,
With a turn of her head
And a lift of her chin
And a gleam of her eye
And a twirl and a spin,
Sailing under
The breathless hush
Of the willows and back
To the frozen rush,
Out to the island
And round the edge,
Skirting the rim
Of the crackling sedge,
Swerving close
To the poplar root
And round the lake
On a single foot,
With a three and an eight
And a loop and a ring;
Where Mary glides,
The lake will sing!
Out in the mist
I hear her now
Under the frost
Of the willow-bough,
Easily sailing,
Light and fleet,
With the song of the lake
Beneath her feet.

*Artist Arthur Burdett Frost captures
the GLORY OF A WINTER'S DAY.
Image By Superstock.*

WHEN CHRISTMAS COMES

Ann D. Lutz

When Christmas comes,
The candles' glow will softly warm the night,
Their flickering beams make angel wings
Of shadows in the light.

When Christmas comes,
The tinselled tree will gleam with
    lights and balls;
The ornaments will glimmer bright
And pine scent fill the halls.

When Christmas comes,
The carols sweet will echo through the air
As voices young and voices old
The joyous notes declare.

When Christmas comes,
The ancient words which tell us of His birth
Will tell again of Bethlehem
Where God came down to earth.

When Christmas comes,
We'll see again the wise men, shepherds, sheep
Around the Christ Child
Mary laid upon the hay to sleep.

When Christmas comes,
God's peace and love will light the world
    with gladness,
And those who live within that light
Will know not death nor sadness.

And so we pray for each and all
As Christmas Eve draws near,
The best of all God's gifts this night
And through the whole new year.

CHRISTMAS

Carolyn Sue Peterson

A golden taper burning on the table,
A pine tree dressed in brightly colored light,
A row of boxes tied with scarlet ribbons,
A single star appearing in the night,

A wreath of evergreens outside the window,
The mistletoe and holly spread galore,
The smoldering branches in the open fireplace,
A group of carolers singing at the door,

The smell of ginger cookies in the oven,
A beaming child that scurries far and near,
The twinkling eyes, the ringing merry laughter—
Oh, Christmas, what a joyous time of year!

The front porch of a bed and breakfast in Indiana offers a merry welcome to all. Photo by Daniel Dempster.

Christmas

Frances Minturn Howard

If the green trees of winter
Moved indoors to houses,
The hemlocks, the cedars,
The spruces, the pines,
Cold in their forests
Moved in by the fire,
Their thick juices warmed
Into pungent sweet scent—
It would smell, yes, it would smell
Like Christmas.

If all of the sounds
Were there for our hearing—
The rustle of tissue,
The clinking of glass,
The small chiming sound
Of the ornaments brushing
One on another,
The ringing of bells—
It would sound, yes, it would sound
Like Christmas.

If globes of thin gold
Dangled before us,
Fragile and brilliant
As fruit of our dreams;
If candles were lighted
Nimbused and flaming,
Touching with splendor
The fruit and the tree—
It would look, yes, it would look
Like Christmas.

But it would not be Christmas—
No, never, not Christmas
Unless there were something
Abroad in the air—
Warmer than snow and
Lighter than raindrops,
A softness, a wonder
That Christmas brings here—
A rebirth, a promise
Large on the air.

The sights and scents of the season are combined in this festive tablescape. Photo by Jessie Walker Associates.

Devotions FROM THE Heart

Pamela Kennedy

Therefore if any man be in Christ, he is a new creature: old things are passed away; behold, all things are become new. 2 Corinthians 5:17

THE GOD OF NEW THINGS

It isn't always easy to accept change. New friends and family members join our circle of relationships; things suddenly aren't the same, and we feel out of balance. We move to a different state or town and the stores and street signs are strange, and we feel uncomfortable. Our financial situation or health alters, and we're worried and concerned. We have to learn to do things differently, and we don't like it.

Holidays seem only to magnify these changes, and we often long for the old, familiar ways. I recall the first Christmas I spent in southern California as a young bride many years ago. I had never before spent a holiday season away from my home and family in the Pacific Northwest. Our tiny tree looked forlorn without the traditional ornaments I had lovingly hung every year. My fruitcake didn't taste quite like Mom's, the turkey wasn't as juicy as hers, and the gravy had unfamiliar lumps. But the worst was the eighty-degree weather and swaying palm trees on Christmas Day! Nothing looked or tasted or even smelled like the holidays. I remember calling home and tearfully complaining, "It isn't Christmas without all the traditions we always shared."

Wisely my mother listened and then gently reminded me, "Then it's time for you to make new traditions."

What great advice! Thirty years and twenty moves later, I've learned the value of embracing new traditions, of welcoming change as a friend instead of resisting it as an enemy. But this approach to life is certainly not unique. In the Bible, God reveals to us that He is a God of new things, of change and movement. He longs to bring us into a new way of life—a new way of thinking about people and places, a new way of accepting the changes He sets before us.

When we refuse to accept change, we refuse to grow. We miss out on wonderful opportunities. We may even miss out on relationships that could bless us in ways we can't imagine. Even a change that brings limitations can be a chance to be still, to listen to God, to allow others to bless us in new ways.

Dear Father, I know I often want things to remain the same, to resist change, to cling to the old ways because they are comfortable. Please help me face the new things You have brought into my life with joyous expectation, trusting in Your unchanging love.

Is there someone new in your family circle this Christmas? Are you living in a new place either physically or emotionally? Are you feeling like the holiday season is just not as special because things aren't the same? Perhaps God is calling you to let Him make all things new for you this year. The precious truth is that even though little in this life remains the same, the Lord emphatically reminds us in the Scriptures, "I am the LORD, I change not" (Malachi 3:6). We can embrace the new things that come our way in confidence that the God who allowed them will remain steadfast. It was His unchanging love that sent the Christ Child so we might experience a new kind of hope. It was His unending grace that provided a Saviour so we could enjoy a new kind of life. We serve a God of new things. This Christmas, rejoice in the newness He brings to you!

The words of the Nativity story add meaning to any Christmas scene. Photo by Daniel Dempster.

Once More

Margaret Rorke

Once more we hear the angels
And hurry from the hills.
Once more the star is shining,
And wisdom through us thrills.
Once more we've come to Christmas.
The spirit of it glows
And fills us each with gladness
No other season knows.

Once more we find the manger
And kneel within our souls
To ask the infant's blessing
Upon our earthly roles.
Once more our love we offer
To Him asleep on hay
And find as we are leaving,
We take more love away.

My Christmas Vow

Ethel Ballard Terry

I shall attend my tasks of love
This year—so that I shall have time
To walk beneath the altar-lit sky
And feel this magic hush sublime
That brings to earth the peace again
Which angels chanted clear that night
To shepherds watching flocks on hills
Of Galilee, beneath strange light.
And, if I'm quiet and listen long,
I too may hear the angels' song!

Eternal Christmas

Elizabeth Stuart Phelps

In the pure soul, although it sing or pray,
The Christ is born anew from day to day;
The life that knoweth Him shall bide apart
And keep eternal Christmas in the heart.

*Artist Linda Nelson Stocks depicts a folk art Christmas
in* Dancing around the Christmas Tree.

The Annunciation

And in the sixth month the angel Gabriel was sent from God unto a city of Galilee, named Nazareth, To a virgin espoused to a man whose name was Joseph, of the house of David; and the virgin's name was Mary.

And the angel came in unto her, and said, Hail, thou that art highly favoured, the Lord is with thee: blessed art thou among women. And when she saw him, she was troubled at his saying, and cast in her mind what manner of salutation this should be.

And the angel said unto her, Fear not, Mary: for thou hast found favour with God. And, behold, thou shalt conceive in thy womb, and bring forth a son, and shalt call his name Jesus. He shall be great, and shall be called the Son of the Highest: and the Lord God shall give unto him the throne of his father David: And he shall reign over the house of Jacob for ever; and of his kingdom there shall be no end.

Then said Mary unto the angel, How shall this be, seeing I know not a man?

And the angel answered and said unto her, The Holy Ghost shall come upon thee, and the power of the Highest shall overshadow thee: therefore also that holy thing which shall be born of thee shall be called the Son of God. For with God nothing shall be impossible.

And Mary said, Behold the handmaid of the Lord; be it unto me according to thy word. And the angel departed from her.

LUKE 1:26–35, 37, 38

THE ANNUNCIATION *by artist Fra Angelico (1387–1455). Taken from the Altarpiece of Montecarlo. S. Maria delle Grazie, S. Giovanni Valdarno, Italy. Image from Scala/Art Resource, New York.*

The Nativity

And it came to pass in those days, that there went out a decree from Caesar Augustus, that all the world should be taxed. (And this taxing was first made when Cyrenius was governor of Syria.) And all went to be taxed, every one into his own city.

And Joseph also went up from Galilee, out of the city of Nazareth, into Judaea, unto the city of David, which is called Bethlehem; (because he was of the house and lineage of David:) To be taxed with Mary his espoused wife, being great with child.

And so it was, that, while they were there, the days were accomplished that she should be delivered. And she brought forth her firstborn son, and wrapped him in swaddling clothes, and laid him in a manger; because there was no room for them in the inn.

LUKE 2:1–7

THE NATIVITY *by artist Fra Angelico (1387–1455). Panel from the Annunziata Silver Chest. Museo di San Marco, Florence, Italy. Image from Scala/Art Resource, New York.*

The Adoration of the Shepherds

And there were in the same country shepherds abiding in the field, keeping watch over their flock by night.

And, lo, the angel of the Lord came upon them, and the glory of the Lord shone round about them: and they were sore afraid. And the angel said unto them, Fear not: for, behold, I bring you good tidings of great joy, which shall be to all people. For unto you is born this day in the city of David a Saviour, which is Christ the Lord. And this shall be a sign unto you; Ye shall find the babe wrapped in swaddling clothes, lying in a manger.

And suddenly there was with the angel a multitude of the heavenly host praising God, and saying, Glory to God in the highest, and on earth peace, good will toward men.

And it came to pass, as the angels were gone away from them into heaven, the shepherds said one to another, Let us now go even unto Bethlehem, and see this thing which is come to pass, which the Lord hath made known unto us. And they came with haste, and found Mary, and Joseph, and the babe lying in a manger.

And when they had seen it, they made known abroad the saying which was told them concerning this child. And all they that heard it wondered at those things which were told them by the shepherds.

But Mary kept all these things, and pondered them in her heart.

And the shepherds returned, glorifying and praising God for all the things that they had heard and seen, as it was told unto them.

LUKE 2:8–20

Detail from THE STORY OF THE LIFE OF CHRIST, ADORATION OF THE MAGI *by artist Fra Angelico (1387–1455). From the Museo di San Marco, Florence, Italy. Image from Superstock.*

The Adoration of the Magi

Now when Jesus was born in Bethlehem of Judaea in the days of Herod the king, behold, there came wise men from the east to Jerusalem, Saying, Where is he that is born King of the Jews? for we have seen his star in the east, and are come to worship him.

Then Herod, when he had privily called the wise men, enquired of them diligently what time the star appeared. And he sent them to Bethlehem, and said, Go and search diligently for the young child; and when ye have found him, bring me word again, that I may come and worship him also.

When they had heard the king, they departed; and, lo, the star, which they saw in the east, went before them, till it came and stood over where the young child was. When they saw the star, they rejoiced with exceeding great joy.

And when they were come into the house, they saw the young child with Mary his mother, and fell down, and worshipped him: and when they had opened their treasures, they presented unto him gifts; gold, and frankincense, and myrrh.

And being warned of God in a dream that they should not return to Herod, they departed into their own country another way.

MATTHEW 2:1, 2, 7–12

THE ADORATION OF THE MAGI *by artist Fra Angelico (1387–1455). Image from Superstock.*

The Flight into Egypt

And when they were departed, behold, the angel of the Lord appeareth to Joseph in a dream, saying, Arise, and take the young child and his mother, and flee into Egypt, and be thou there until I bring thee word: for Herod will seek the young child to destroy him.

When he arose, he took the young child and his mother by night, and departed into Egypt: And was there until the death of Herod: that it might be fulfilled which was spoken of the Lord by the prophet, saying, Out of Egypt have I called my son.

MATTHEW 2:13–15

THE STORY OF THE LIFE OF CHRIST, THE FLIGHT TO EGYPT *by artist Fra Angelico (1387–1455). From the Museo di San Marco, Florence, Italy. Image from Superstock.*

A Christmas Eve Choral

Bliss Carman

Hallelujah!
What sound is this across the dark
While all the earth is sleeping? Hark!
Hallelujah! Hallelujah! Hallelujah!

Why are thy tender eyes so bright,
Mary, Mary?
"On the prophetic deep of night,
Joseph, Joseph,
I see the borders of the light,
And in the day that is to be
An aureoled man-child I see,
Great love's son, Joseph.
Hallelujah!"
He hears not, but she hears afar
The minstrel angel of the star.
Hallelujah! Hallelujah! Hallelujah!

Why is thy gentle smile so deep,
Mary, Mary?
"It is the secret I must keep,
Joseph, Joseph,
The joy that will not let me sleep,
The glory of the coming days,
When all the world shall turn to praise
God's goodness, Joseph.
Hallelujah!"
Clear as the bird that brings the morn
She hears the heavenly music borne.
Hallelujah! Hallelujah! Hallelujah!

Why is thy voice so strange and far,
Mary, Mary?
"I see the glory of the star,
Joseph, Joseph,
And in its light all things that are
Made glad and wise beyond the sway
Of death and darkness and dismay,
In God's time, Joseph.
Hallelujah!"
To every heart in love 'tis given
To hear the ecstasy of heaven.
Hallelujah! Hallelujah! Hallelujah!

O Simplicitas

Madeleine L'Engle

An angel came to me
And I was unprepared
To be what God was using.
Mother I was to be.
A moment I despaired,
Thought briefly of refusing.
The angel knew I heard.
According to God's Word
I bowed to this strange choosing.

A palace should have been
The birthplace of a king
(I had no way of knowing).
We went to Bethlehem;
It was so strange a thing.
The wind was cold, and blowing,
My cloak was old, and thin.
They turned us from the inn;
The town was overflowing.

God's Word, a child so small,
Who still must learn to speak,
Lay in humiliation.
Joseph stood, strong and tall.
The beasts were warm and meek
And moved with hesitation.
The Child born in a stall?
I understood it: all.
Kings came in adoration.

Perhaps it was absurd:
The stable set apart,
The sleepy cattle lowing;
And the incarnate Word
Resting against my heart.
My joy was overflowing.
The shepherds came, adored
The folly of the Lord,
Wiser than all men's knowing.

From My Garden Journal

Deana Deck

STAR-OF-BETHLEHEM

I spotted the flower called star-of-Bethlehem for the first time several years ago, nestled among the colorful drifts of spring wildflowers that festooned the neighborhood around my new home. Their stunning white color, displayed in thick blankets among the trees, quickly caught my eye. Unfamiliar with these cheerful plants, I began asking neighbors what they were and soon discovered that these clumps of blossoms with crocus-like foliage were known as star-of-Bethlehem. Feeling that the mystery had been solved, I didn't give much more thought to the topic until recently, when a reader asked me how to recreate the blooming pots of star-of-Bethlehem she had seen used as centerpieces at a Christmas wedding. I was intrigued by the possibility that the plant I had known only as a wild, spring bloomer could be forced to bloom indoors, and in the wintertime, no less; so I set out to uncover the history of the star-of-Bethlehem and its unique name.

When I began researching this tiny spring flower, I discovered that far from being a wildflower, which is what I thought I was dealing with, star-of-Bethlehem is a bulb plant. Horticulturalists identified it in the late sixteenth century; and because it is a native of North Africa, it may very well have traveled to Europe with the Crusaders. Sources seem to vary on the origin of the name, but it's easy to picture a Christian knight, longing for the pomp and pageantry of a European Christmas, coming upon this delicate plant and naming it for the brightest of stars.

Although star-of-Bethlehem was first classified hundreds of years ago, it has never received the worldwide frenzy such as that which greeted that Turkish wonder, the tulip. Exotic North African bulbs were not in great demand, and the availability of star-of-Bethlehem remained limited. Today's gardener, however, is lucky to have nurseries that specialize in bulbs and carry several varieties of star-of-Bethlehem. The most common variety is *Ornithagalum umbellatum*, which blooms in April and early May. This species grows equally well in sun or partial shade, and its white blooms sport pale green stripes on the undersides of the petals. Flowers appear in clusters with stems nine to twelve inches long, and the plant is hardy to Zone 6. Farther north, the bulbs can be container grown.

Another star-of-Bethlehem species is *O. thyrsoides*, which is also called "chincherinchee" by those who have discovered its beauty and liveliness. This southern plant, hardy only to Zone 8, has tight clusters of blooms atop each single stalk and makes an excellent cut flower, living two to three weeks in water. Chincherinchee is also a good choice for drying and is one of the few flowers that seems to dry better after opening in water.

O. nutans, which is also called Silver Bells, resembles its cousins, except that the star-shaped petals curve outward and give the blossoms a bell-like appearance. Its flowers can be up to two inches in diameter, as compared with those of O. umbellatum which are seldom more than one inch wide. A newcomer to the group, having only been in cultivation since 1884, is O. balansae, a dwarf species that blooms in March and April. It too sports pale green on the petals' undersides.

All of these bulbs are easy to grow and are free of diseases and pests. Some naturalize so readily that they are considered invasive in a formal flower bed. Scattered around the yard and under tall trees, however, they make a beautiful spring display. To create drifts of color, dig out a large area about an inch deep and scatter the small bulbs before replacing the soil. The plants demand good drainage and a somewhat sandy soil (a vestige of their North African heritage), so it is wise to amend the bed with sandy loam, sand and leaf mold, or compost before planting. Water moderately when growth begins and more freely in full growth, unless you are blessed with abundant spring rains. An occasional dose of manure tea will keep your drifts of star-of-Bethlehem well-nourished and produce the most vivid displays in spring.

To many people, like my questioning reader, star-of-Bethlehem's perfect six-pointed, star-shaped flowers may look most beautiful at Christmastime; so to force the blooms indoors in time for the holidays, begin around the third week of August and plant several pots in relays, each a week later than the previous one since forcing is not an exact science. Using a loose, well-draining mixture of one part loam, one part peat, and one part sand, plant five or six bulbs in each pot. Be sure the pots have a drainage hole in the bottom. If you live where winters are cold, you can put them into cold frames; otherwise you'll need to store the pots in an unheated shed or chill them in the refrigerator. The bulbs need to be kept moist and at a temperature below forty-eight degrees for thirteen weeks. A vigorous root system will develop which, depending on the size of the container, may be visible through the drainage holes. They may also begin putting up green shoots. After the required period of chilling, bring the container into a warm room with bright light. In about four weeks the plants should begin to bloom, hopefully just in time to become delightful centerpieces for your own Christmas party.

I'm glad that a reader's intriguing question led me to discover more about the star-of-Bethlehem. Perhaps it is beginning to receive a bit of the popularity it deserves after reminding gardeners of the Christmas star for so many years. I still eagerly await the beautiful drifts of star-of-Bethlehem that greet me each spring; but on consideration, I think I have come to appreciate the December blooms even more. After all, I don't mind seeing these lovely blooms two seasons each year, and what better time than Christmas to enjoy the pure-white flower named for the brightest of stars?

What better time than Christmas to enjoy the pure-white flower named for the brightest of stars?

Deana Deck tends to her flowers, plants, and vegetables at her home in Nashville, Tennessee, where her popular garden column is a regular feature in The Tennessean.

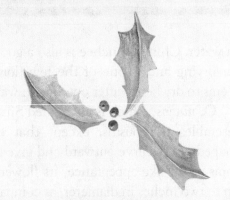

GOING HOME

LaVerne P. Larson

I'm going home for Christmas,
To that lovely place aglow
With a special magic splendor
I have always treasured so.

I'm going home for Christmas,
Where love waits at the door
And my heart is ever welcome
To share happiness in store.

I'm going home for Christmas,
Across the sparkling snow,
To hear stories, bells, and carols
And bask in candleglow.

I'm going home for Christmas
To help trim the Christmas tree
And give gifts to all my loved ones
Who mean so much to me.

I'm going home for Christmas
Because I love it there;
Its open arms envelop me
With blessings I may share.

HOME FOR CHRISTMAS

Rosalene Guingrich

Oh, let there be joy
In the old home tonight,
A tree in the window
With soft candlelight.
And let there be music,
Some glad smiles and mirth
For those who still gather
Around the old hearth.

Oh, let there be garlands
And firelight's glow,
The warmth of affection
Where bitter winds blow.

'Tis good to hear laughter
And bursts of delight
For homey gifts hung
On the tree Christmas night.

In my heart is the spirit
Of days long gone by,
And I long to play Santa
As Christmas draws nigh.

Home ties are calling,
And tapers burn bright;
Let me rush home for Christmas
With childish delight!

*A home in Warwick, New York, is prepared for the coming
of Christmas. Image by Scott Barrow/International Stock.*

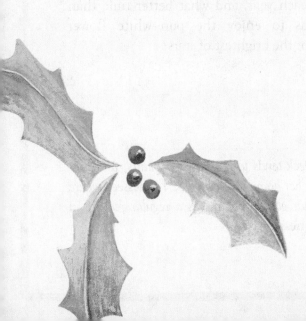

BABY'S FIRST CHRISTMAS

Marion Purdy

I remember her first Christmas;
It was just like yesterday,
Though she didn't know the meaning
In her little baby way.
She just clasped her hands together,
Wore a look of sweet surprise,
And I saw the whole of Christmas
There reflected in her eyes.

TO MY SON ON HIS FIRST CHRISTMAS

Carol B. Parker

Tiny baby, sleeping tight
On this the world's most glorious night;
How I wish that you could know
The radiance that you bestow
On your first, silent Christmas Eve.
As you lie dreaming on my sleeve
I think about that other boy
Whose birth brought all men such great joy.
His mother must have held Him thus
And rocked Him so He wouldn't fuss
When strangers, shepherds, came to say
Welcome to the Child who lay
In a stable dark and rude
Where the angels said He would.

My son, you have so much more than He
Did then—a home, a bed—but we
Can only hope that you will be
A little like the Man that He
Became—kind and good and brave,
Happy to give His life to save
His fellowmen. So, baby, sleep,
That you may grow and learn to keep
The faith that holy Child brought then
In peace on earth, good will to men.

Some Christmas gifts are more precious than others, as seen in Kathryn Andrews Fincher's THE BEST GIFT. Image copyright © Arts Uniq Inc., Cookeville, Tennessee.

Christmas Eve

Helen Welshimer

It is so still tonight, and far away,
So far sometimes men do not see it now.
A gold star shines through dream-swept ages,
And wise men come, and wondering shepherds bow.

It is so still, the years are amber-lighted
By softened magic where a star once hung,
And down the windy highways there comes drifting
The fluted song that angels' throats have sung.

A song—Judea did not hear it;
She pulled her blinds, put out her quiet lights,
And went to bed so early that far evening;
How could she tell this was the night of nights?

The song comes back, low-voiced tonight and pleading,
Across a field where shepherd bands are still.
Is there no way through trails of purple centuries
That I may take to bring me to that hill?

I cannot call it fancy nor an idle whim
That makes me search on Christmas Eve for Him.

Christmas is a quest.
May each of us follow
his star of faith and find
the heart's own Bethlehem.

—ESTHER BALDWIN YORK

Christmas Eve

Eugenia Congo

Can any time compare to Christmas Eve,
When days of frantic shopping tours are past,
When trees are trimmed and presents
      gaily wrapped,
And you can breathe a happy sigh at last?
When, glancing at the knobby silhouettes
Of stockings hung against the ember glow,
You reach for Santa's milk and cookie snack
As strains of "Silent Night" play soft and low?

Is any hour so dear on Christmas Eve
As when your little flock is safe asleep,
And all alone you hear the angels' song,
Bringing a joy you shall forever keep?
When, window-gazing past the candle-beam,
You seek a radiance the shepherds viewed
And pray all weary mothers on this night
May share the peace of this sweet interlude?

Can any moment match the worth of this,
A gift not sold in any busy mart,
This priceless moment when the holy Child
Is born anew within the quiet heart?
Now fresh upon the ear glad tidings sound,
The season's fret and frenzy to condemn,
As neath the tree's symbolic star you feel
You have, yourself, knelt down in Bethlehem.

A candlelit room offers an ideal spot to relish the precious
hours of Christmas Eve. Photo by Jessie Walker Associates.

BITS & PIECES

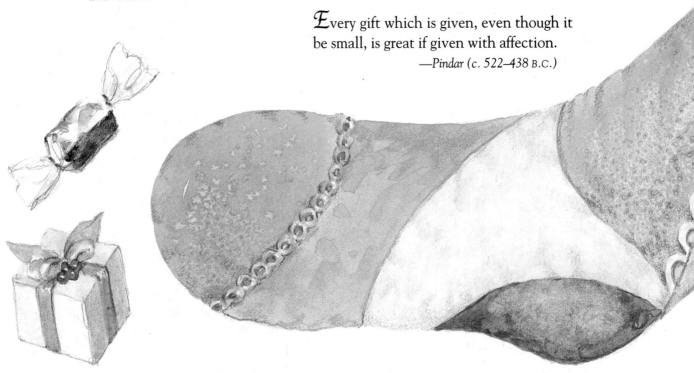

Welcome, Christmas! heel and toe,
Here we wait thee in a row. . . .
Fill us quickly ere you go,
Fill us till we overflow.
—*Mary Mapes Dodge*

Give unto all, lest he whom thou deny'st
May chance to be no other man but Christ.
—*Robert Herrick*

Not he who has much is rich,
but he who gives much.
—*Erich Fromm*

Every gift which is given, even though it
be small, is great if given with affection.
—*Pindar (c. 522–438 B.C.)*

Somehow, not only for Christmas
But all the long year through,
The joy that you give to others
Is the joy that comes back to you.
—*John Greenleaf Whittier*

My good will is great,
though the gift is small.
—*William Shakespeare*

The only gift is a portion of thyself.
—Ralph Waldo Emerson

What is a true gift? One for which nothing is expected in return.
—Chinese Proverb

As the purse is emptied, the heart is filled.
—Victor Hugo

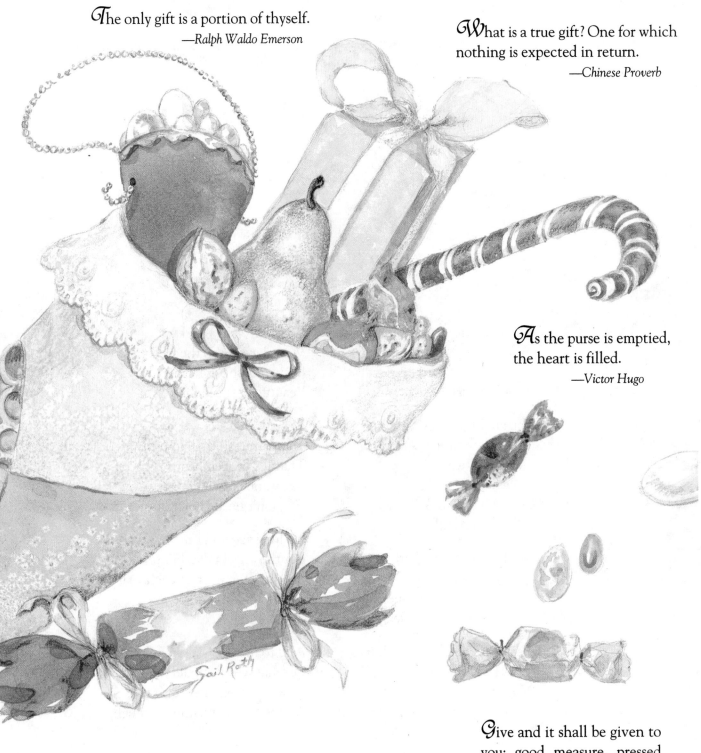

Give and it shall be given to you; good measure, pressed down, and shaken together, and running over.
—Luke 6:38

Do you see this ragged stocking,
Here a rent and there a hole?
Each thread of this little stocking
Is woven around my soul.
—Frances E. W. Harper

A gift, however small, speaks its own language.
—Norman Vincent Peale

Readers' Reflections

A Simple Christmas

Helen Gregory
Florissant, Missouri

Our Christmas was quite simple
With stockings neatly hung;
Mama smiled with approval
As all the carols were sung.

Papa held the tree upright;
We had no proper stand,
But bits of wood
    would do us fine.
And the tree looked
    oh, so grand.

We had one box of ornaments,
And we used them every year.
Yet each one was so special;
Each one to me was dear.

Papa strung the tree with lights.
The tinsel then was next.
No matter it got shorter
From one Christmas to the next!

A tiny broken angel
Was placed atop the tree.
Each year she grew more
Beautiful, especially to me.

Perhaps that she was broken
Taught me all the more
That it's broken hearts
    we need to mend;
We don't need gifts from stores.

It's long ago and time has passed,
But the angel takes her place;
She sits atop my tree each year
With her cracked but
    beaming face.

And to me she is a symbol
Of what we all should do;
Open wide our arms of love,
And let the light shine through.

Editor's Note: Readers are invited to submit original poetry for possible publication in future issues of Ideals. *Please send typed copies only; manuscripts will not be returned. Writers receive $10 for each published submission. Send material to Readers' Reflections, Ideals Publications, 535 Metroplex Drive, Suite 250, Nashville, Tennessee 37211.*

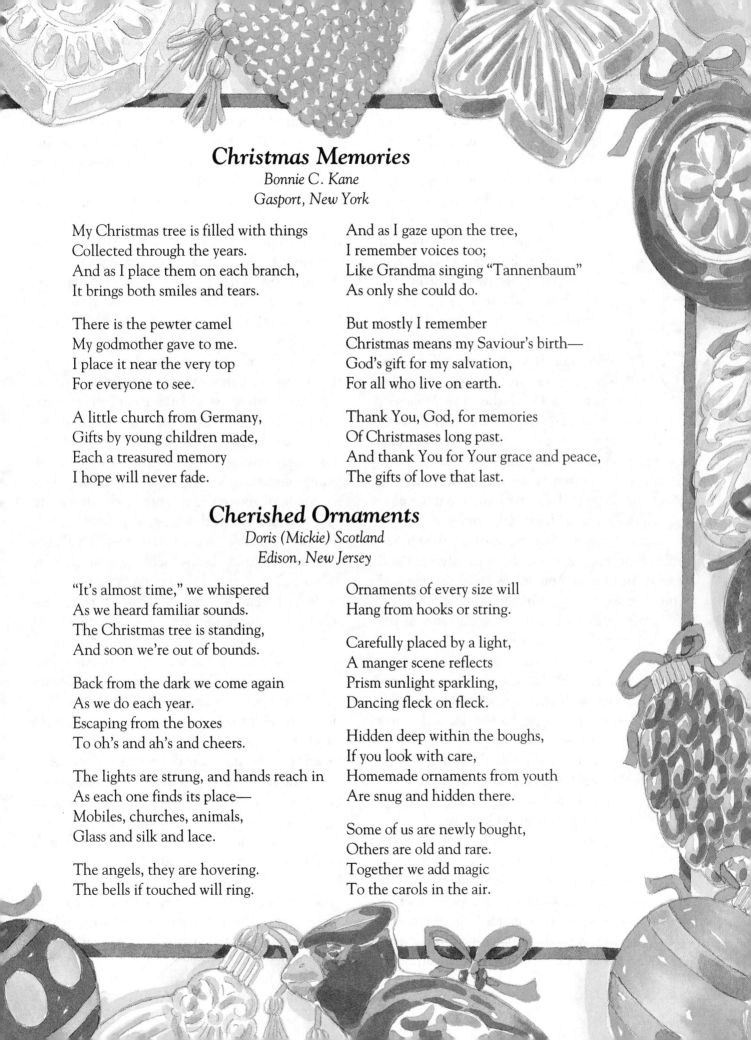

Christmas Memories

Bonnie C. Kane
Gasport, New York

My Christmas tree is filled with things
Collected through the years.
And as I place them on each branch,
It brings both smiles and tears.

There is the pewter camel
My godmother gave to me.
I place it near the very top
For everyone to see.

A little church from Germany,
Gifts by young children made,
Each a treasured memory
I hope will never fade.

And as I gaze upon the tree,
I remember voices too;
Like Grandma singing "Tannenbaum"
As only she could do.

But mostly I remember
Christmas means my Saviour's birth—
God's gift for my salvation,
For all who live on earth.

Thank You, God, for memories
Of Christmases long past.
And thank You for Your grace and peace,
The gifts of love that last.

Cherished Ornaments

Doris (Mickie) Scotland
Edison, New Jersey

"It's almost time," we whispered
As we heard familiar sounds.
The Christmas tree is standing,
And soon we're out of bounds.

Back from the dark we come again
As we do each year.
Escaping from the boxes
To oh's and ah's and cheers.

The lights are strung, and hands reach in
As each one finds its place—
Mobiles, churches, animals,
Glass and silk and lace.

The angels, they are hovering.
The bells if touched will ring.

Ornaments of every size will
Hang from hooks or string.

Carefully placed by a light,
A manger scene reflects
Prism sunlight sparkling,
Dancing fleck on fleck.

Hidden deep within the boughs,
If you look with care,
Homemade ornaments from youth
Are snug and hidden there.

Some of us are newly bought,
Others are old and rare.
Together we add magic
To the carols in the air.

COLLECTOR'S CORNER

BLOWN-GLASS ORNAMENTS

Amy Johnson

When I was nine years old, my Christmas gift from my grandmother was a blown-glass ornament to hang on our family's Christmas tree. Having just moved to the United States from London, I was eager to fit in with the other kids at school, and my Christmas list included new clothes, a softball glove, and a cassette player. I could not help but be disappointed when I opened the box from my grandmother and found the glass ornament shaped like a bird. I grudgingly thanked her for the gift and hung it on one of our tree's branches. But despite my attempts to remain ambivalent about the ornament, I slowly became enthralled with the story Grandmother shared with me about her family's association with blown-glass ornaments.

Like me, my grandmother came to the United States from Europe when she was only nine and viewed the trip to America as both exciting and somewhat frightening. Grandmother was born to German parents in Lauscha, a small town in the eastern part of Germany, where her father continued a long family tradition of creating blown-glass ornaments. Although Lauscha was a major production center of blown-glass ornaments in the early 1920s, my great-grandfather decided it was best to leave his business behind and seek a better life for his family in America. In the spring of 1929 Grandmother and her family came to America and brought with them the ornaments that had been such a big part of their lives in Germany.

Once they arrived in America, my great-grandfather worked as a shoe salesman but continued to make blown-glass ornaments in his spare time. My grandmother helped paint and decorate the ornaments once they had been molded. She continued to help her family produce blown-glass ornaments until after she finished school and was married. It wasn't until thirty years later, after my parents and I moved to the United States, that Grandmother decided to give away some of her ornaments. By this point, her collection contained at least one hundred blown-glass ornaments, from simple glass globes to animals to an intricately designed church that reminded her of the one she had attended in Germany as a child. She wanted to make sure that the recipient of these treasures would value them as much as she. Because she saw similarities between her life and my own, Grandmother chose to give her ornaments to me.

A tradition was born that Christmas of my ninth year, one that my grandmother continued until her death ten years later. Each year my ornament collection increased with the addition of a few more fascinating pieces. One of my favorites was made by my great-grandfather shortly after his family came to America and is shaped like a bear in honor of former President Teddy Roosevelt. The bear ornament, though it is quite old, is not the most valuable of my collectibles. That prize goes to a delicate globe that dates from the late 1800s and encases a scene of the Nativity. It was made by a famous German craftsman who mentored my great-grandfather.

I am fortunate to own many beautiful ornaments that once belonged to my grandmother; and since her death, I have purchased several vintage blown-glass ornaments to add to my collection. One of my favorites is shaped like an angel; another is an intricately painted gold star and was found at an antique store during my college years.

Although the ornaments I purchase for myself can never equal the precious ornaments my grandmother gave me, I still enjoy searching for new additions to my collection. Grandmother's memory lives on in the ornaments she has given me. Each Christmas, as I hang my colorful ornaments on the tree, I think of the full life my grandmother lived and of the lifelong appreciation she has instilled in me for blown-glass ornaments.

ORNAMENTAL INFORMATION

If you are interested in collecting blown-glass Christmas ornaments, the following information may be helpful:

HISTORY

• The Egyptians invented the art of glassblowing over five thousand years ago.

• Although Germany was the European center of glassmaking from the late 1500s to the end of World War II, several other European countries, including Poland and Czechoslovakia, also produced blown-glass ornaments.

• In 1848 glassblowers first learned how to blow glass into molds to create specific shapes.

• The art of glassblowing was not perfected until 1867, when glassblowers discovered how to control the intensity of a flame, thus ensuring that the glass would be melted properly.

• F. W. Woolworth, founder of a chain of stores bearing his name, began making trips to Lauscha to search for ornaments in the latter part of the 1800s. He marketed the first blown-glass ornaments in America in 1890.

GLASSBLOWING TECHNIQUES

• Before glass can be blown, it has to melt at a temperature of 2100° F. The glass is heated in a furnace and then stored in a holding area to keep it hot until it is ready to be blown.

• Glassblowing involves placing a bubble of molten glass into the bottom half of a mold, closing the top of the mold over the hot glass, and blowing air through a tube into the mold to expand the glass inside. Within only a few seconds, the mold is opened and the glass inside has conformed to the shape of the mold.

• In nineteenth-century Europe, glassblowing was often a family affair, with the father blowing the glass, the mother decorating the finished product, and the children painting simple designs on the ornaments.

TIPS FOR COLLECTORS

• More popular vintage designs of blown-glass ornaments include birdhouses and animals. Birds,

These two blown-glass ornaments are examples of modern ornaments using nineteenth-century methods and vintage molds. Images courtesy Merck Family's Old World Christmas, Spokane, Washington.

because they belong in trees and thus are popular at Christmastime, are some of the most sought-after ornaments for collectors.

• Collectors of blown-glass ornaments should learn to distinguish between old and new ornaments. Older ornaments often weigh less than new ones and have a very thin glass wall.

• Collectors are typically drawn to turn-of-the-century German ornaments, which tend to consist of more delicate glass, have more intricate detail, and be made from more unique molds than ornaments crafted in the United States.

• To reach collector's status, a blown-glass ornament should be made from a vintage mold.

• Unless they are old or extremely rare, ornaments that are cracked, damaged, or missing paint will be dramatically decreased in value.

A SONG OF THE SNOW

Madison J. Cawein

Roaring winds that rocked the crow,
　　High in his eyrie,
All night long, and to and fro
Swung the cedar and drove the snow
Out of the North, have ceased to blow;
　　And dawn breaks fiery.
Sing, Ho, a song of the winter dawn,
When the air is still and the clouds are gone,
And the snow lies deep on hill and lawn,
　　And the old clock ticks, 'Tis time! 'Tis time!
And the household rises with many a yawn—
Sing, Ho, a song of the winter dawn!
　　Sing Ho!

Deep in the East a ruddy glow
　　Broadens and brightens,
Glints through the icicles, row on row,
Flames on the panes of the farmhouse low,
And over the miles of drifted snow
　　Silently whitens.
Sing, Ho, a song of the winter sky,
When the last star closes its icy eye,
And deep in the road the snow-drifts lie,
　　And the old clock ticks, 'Tis late! 'Tis late!
And the flame on the hearth leaps red, leaps high—
Sing, Ho, a song of the winter sky!
　　Sing Ho!

Into the heav'n the sun comes slow,
　　All red and frowzy;
Out of the shed the muffled low
Of the cattle comes; and the rooster's crow
Sounds strangely distant beneath the snow
　　And dull and drowsy.
Sing, Ho, a song of the winter morn,
When the snow makes ghostly the wayside thorn,
And hills of pearl are the shocks of corn,
　　And the old clock ticks, Tick-tock, tick-tock;
And the goodman bustles about the barn—
Sing, Ho, a song of the winter morn!
　　Sing Ho!

Now to their tasks the farmhands go,
　　Cheerily, cheerily:
The maid with her pail, her cheeks aglow;
And, blowing his fist, the man with his hoe
To trample a path through the crunching snow,
　　Merrily, merrily.
Sing, Ho, a song of the winter day,
When ermine-capped are the stacks of hay,
And the wood-smoke pillars the air with gray,
　　And the old clock ticks, To work! lo work!
And the goodwife sings as she churns away—
Sing, Ho, a song of the winter day!
　　Sing Ho!

A barn stands amid the snow in Finley, Oregon. Photo by Dennis Frates/Oregon Scenics.

LEGENDARY AMERICANS

Lisa C. Ragan

HENRY WADSWORTH LONGFELLOW

W hen Henry Wadsworth Longfellow was born on February 27, 1807, American poetry was in its infancy. The country was young and still looked to Europe for the best in literature, which meant that no American poet during those years was able to earn a living solely by writing poetry. With Longfellow's birth, however, the status of American literature would soon change. Though unbeknownst to the country at the time, America's first poet laureate had been born.

Often I think of the beautiful town
That is seated by the sea;

Often in thought go up and down
The pleasant streets of that dear old town,
And my youth comes back to me.

Born in Portland, Maine, Longfellow would later write with fondness of the busy seaport and the New England countryside where he grew up. The second of eight children, Longfellow was fortunate to be born into comfortable wealth and privilege. Both his father and his maternal grandfather were no-nonsense congressmen; but his mother, Zilpah, instilled in the children a love of literature and a religious idealism that would color Longfellow's later writing.

Young Henry excelled at the private Portland Academy school he attended. At age thirteen, he published his first poem in the local newspaper, and by age fourteen, he enrolled in Bowdoin College and began to study languages and literature. By the time of his graduation from Bowdoin at age eighteen, Longfellow's zeal had caught the attention of his professors. The trustees offered him a professorship in modern languages, a newly created position that required study in Europe for three years. Thus began Longfellow's twenty-five-year teaching career—first at Bowdoin College in Maine and later as the Smith Professor of Modern Languages at Harvard.

Tell me not, in mournful numbers,
Life is but an empty dream!
For the soul is dead that slumbers,
And things are not what they seem.

In 1831, Longfellow married a hometown girl and former classmate at Portland Academy named Mary Storer Potter. It was with Mary that he sailed to Europe for the second time to study languages before embarking upon his teaching career at Harvard. While overseas, Mary miscarried their first child and died from the resulting infection. Distraught and alone, Longfellow suffered a deep depression following his wife's death. Although he continued his studies in Europe, his heart was heavy with the loss.

The following spring found Longfellow at Interlaken where he met fellow New Englander Nathan Appleton and his family. Longfellow's spirits lifted as he visited with Nathan Appleton's daughter Frances, an intelligent, talented, and beautiful young woman. He fell in love with her, and his feelings remained steadfast despite her early rejection of him. Romantic fervor prompted Longfellow to write the novel *Hyperion*, an account of young lovers who meet in Switzerland and the lady's subsequent rejection of her suitor. Far too familiar with the subject, Frances Appleton, Fanny, was incensed upon reading the novel, and her ire placed a wall between them for some years. In fact, seven years passed before her heart softened and she consented to become Longfellow's wife.

During the years of his slow return to Fanny's favor, Longfellow settled into teaching at Harvard and took up residence at Craigie House, a historic home that had provided sanctuary to George Washington during the British seige of Boston. The comfortable elegance of Craigie House suited him and became his home for the rest of his life. Without Fanny, Longfellow poured his passion into his poetry and began to publish more, including "The Village Blacksmith" and "The Wreck of *Hesperus*." Always keenly aware of current events, Longfellow was ardently opposed to slavery and wrote a number of anti-slavery poems. His interest in teaching waned as his love of writing poetry grew. Whereas he enjoyed his students and displayed talent as a lecturer, Longfellow craved more time to devote to his writing. But soon the poet's limited time had to be shared with family as well.

> *I have you fast in my fortress,*
> *And will not let you depart,*
> *But put you down into the dungeon*
> *In the round-tower of my heart.*

Longfellow and Fanny were wed in 1843, and a harmonious bliss soon enveloped the couple. Fanny's wealthy father, Nathan Appleton, bought Craigie House and presented it to the couple as a wedding present. They were blessed with six children, losing one little girl before her second birthday. Longfellow enjoyed fatherhood and took interest in his children's lives, immortalizing his three little girls in "The Children's Hour." As his children grew, Longfellow continued to publish;

and by 1854, he resigned from Harvard and began to support his family solely as an American poet.

> *By the shores of Gitche Gumee,*
> *By the shining Big-Sea-Water,*
> *Stood the wigwam of Nokomis,*
> *Daughter of the Moon, Nokomis.*

Longfellow had maintained a sincere interest in the history and lives of Native Americans since his college days; and shortly after retiring from teaching, he wrote *The Song of Hiawatha*, which by 1860 had sold fifty thousand copies. His popularity with American readers was unprecedented. With his treatment of distinctly American subjects such as Hiawatha, Evangeline, and Paul Revere, he soon became known as America's unofficial poet laureate.

The summer of 1861 brought tragedy to the Longfellow household. Fanny was sealing packets of their daughters' hair with hot wax (a Victorian tradition) when her dress caught fire and engulfed her in flames. She ran to Henry in the next room, and in his efforts to stop the fire, he became seriously burned himself. Fanny did not survive the accident, and Longfellow's face became so badly scarred that he wore a beard for the rest of his life. Never to marry again, Longfellow devoted his remaining years to raising his children and to writing his poetry.

> *Under a spreading chestnut-tree*
> *The village smithy stands;*
> *The smith, a mighty man is he,*
> *With large and sinewy hands . . .*

Longfellow's later years were filled with honors. On his seventy-second birthday, the children of Cambridge presented Longfellow with an armchair crafted from the wood of the original chestnut tree, forever remembered in "The Village Blacksmith." On his last trip to Europe he received honorary degrees from Oxford and Cambridge universities and a reception from Queen Victoria. Writing poetry until the end of his life, Longfellow completed "The Bells of San Blas" just nine days before his death at age seventy-five. The work of America's unofficial first poet laureate remains one of the greatest treasures of American literature.

LONGFELLOW NATIONAL HISTORIC SITE
CAMBRIDGE, MASSACHUSETTS
Elizabeth Bonner Kea

Henry Wadsworth Longfellow has long been considered one of the most influential and widely read poets in North America and Europe. Like every school child, I was introduced to Longfellow at a young age; but not until later, when my literary tastes had developed, did I truly appreciate his poetic works and the contribution he had made to American literary history. As a lover of literature, and Longfellow's in particular, it was only natural that, during a visit to Cambridge at Christmas three years ago, I visit the setting in which this literary giant thrived for forty-five years.

I arrived at the Longfellow National Historic Site at dusk; and as I made my way up the walk leading to the house, I admired the mid-Georgian architecture framing the structure that contained more than two hundred years of history. Built in 1759 by Major John Vassall, a wealthy Royalist who fled to England on the eve of the American Revolution, the house had lodged several prominent figures even before Longfellow began his residence in 1837. George Washington, while serving as commander in chief of the Continental army and overseeing the siege of Boston, stayed here from April 1775 to March 1776. The house then passed through the hands of two wealthy Bostonians before becoming the property of Andrew Craigie in 1791. Craigie enlarged the house with two piazzas and a large ell and constructed Cambridge's first icehouse and greenhouse on the grounds.

Upon her husband's death in 1819, Mrs. Craigie assumed responsibility for the house and, in order to pay off debts, began renting rooms to Harvard University professors and students. In 1837 Henry Wadsworth Longfellow, recently appointed as Professor of Modern Languages at Harvard, became one of those tenants. Six years later, Longfellow's father-in-law, Nathaniel Appleton, who understood the fondness his son-in-law had for the house, purchased the estate as a wedding gift for his daughter, Fanny Appleton, and Longfellow. After Mrs. Longfellow's death in 1861, the poet continued to reside here with his five children and wrote prolifically until his own death in 1882. In 1962, eighty years after the poet's death, Congress passed legislation authorizing the acquisition of Longfellow National Historic Site "in order to preserve ownership for the benefit and inspiration of the people of the United States."

As I entered the house that evening, my sense of its historical significance only increased. In celebration of the holidays, garland entwined the columns and candles filled the rooms with a soft glow, capturing the mood of a Victorian Christmas—just as Longfellow and his family might have known. As I toured the seventeen restored rooms, I admired the historical furnishings as well as the nineteenth-century paintings and sculptures. Excerpts from Longfellow's writings came to mind; and I pictured "descending the broad hall stair, / grave Alice, and laughing Allegra, / and Edith with golden hair." Much of the spirit of the family still remained: sketches by the children, a small table-top Christmas tree similar to that which the Longfellows displayed annually, paintings of Longfellow's closest friends, and a library collection of ten thousand

Henry Wadsworth Longfellow's Cambridge home is framed by ice-covered trees after a winter storm. Photo courtesy of the National Park Service, Longfellow National Historic Site.

leather-bound books.

I had walked past the study as I entered the Great Hall; but anticipating the study more than any room in the house, I chose to tour it last. Situated next to the window overlooking the Charles River stood a high desk where Longfellow wrote in the early morning before the house came alive with the bustling of children. Such works as *Evangeline, The Song of Hiawatha, The Courtship of Miles Standish,* and "The Midnight Ride of Paul Revere" were composed there. At the opposite wall two chairs faced a small fireplace and seemed to invite guests to gather and chat. I could hardly imagine the philosophical and literary ideas discussed at this fireside as Longfellow hosted other literary giants, including Dickens, Hawthorne, and Emerson.

I turned to leave, but paused, perhaps feeling the same reluctance Longfellow felt long ago: "See the fire is sinking low, / dusky red the embers glow, / while above them I still cower, / while a moment more I linger." At the doorway, I stood for a moment longer as well, hoping to glean any literary inspiration still wafting in the air. As I exited the house, I felt my visit to the Longfellow National Historic Site had offered new insight into the life of one of America's most beloved poets.

Where Christmas Comes

Minnie Klemme

Christmas comes to town and country,
Comes to hamlet and to farm
With its special brand of gladness
And its special kind of charm.

Christmas comes to range and seaboard,
To the outposts of the world;
Comes to every tongue and nation
Where Christ's banner is unfurled.

Christmas comes to home and hovel,
To the mansion great and fine,
To the cabin and the cottage,
To the palm tree and the pine.

Christmas comes to city churches
With their spires and their domes;
Comes to humble parish churches
Where the poor folks have their homes.

Christmas comes because the Christ Child
Came to save the world from sin.
Listen to the church bells ringing
Joy without and peace within.

Christmas Links the World

Katherine Edelman

Christmas links the world today,
Countries new and old,
As round the hearthfires of the earth
The story of the Christ Child's birth
Is reverently told.

Christmas links the world today.
We hear its sweet, glad call
As hymns held lovingly by time,
As carols, bells, and sounding chime
Bring Bethlehem to all.

*Christmas is not a time or a season, but a state of mind.
To cherish peace and good will, to be plenteous in mercy,
is to have the real spirit of Christmas. If we think o'er
these things, there will be born in us a Saviour and over
us will shine a star sending its gleam of hope to the world.*

—Calvin Coolidge

An age-old doorway in Rothenberg, Germany, displays the international spirit of Christmas. Photo by H. Armstrong Roberts.

Ideals' Family Recipes

Whether it's a German grandmother's strudel or a favorite recipe from an overseas trip, we borrow holiday cooking traditions from all over the world to make Christmas "ours." Why not borrow from your heritage this Christmas, perhaps with one of the following sweets with an international flair? Mail a typed copy of your own favorite recipe along with your name, address, and phone number to Ideals Magazine, ATTN: Recipes, 535 Metroplex Drive, Suite 250, Nashville, Tennessee 37211. We will pay $10 for each recipe chosen.

Swedish Spice Cookies

Kim Bennett of Raleigh, North Carolina

1 teaspoon ground mace
½ teaspoon ground ginger
1 cup butter, softened

½ cup granulated sugar
1 egg yolk
2 teaspoons vanilla extract

2½ cups all-purpose flour
Powdered sugar

Preheat oven to 350° F. In a large bowl, combine first 6 ingredients. Blend until fluffy. Gradually stir in flour. Put dough through a cookie press, using the broad plate, onto an ungreased cookie sheet. Bake 10 minutes or until cookies have browned slightly around the edges. Cool on wire rack. Roll in powdered sugar. Makes 3½ dozen cookies.

Spiced French Madeleines

Melanee Gentry of Memphis, Tennessee

1¼ cups cake flour
½ teaspoon baking powder
¼ teaspoon salt
½ teaspoon ground mace

⅛ teaspoon ground cardamom
3 eggs
⅔ cup granulated sugar
2 teaspoons grated lemon rind

1 cup butter, melted
and divided
Powdered sugar

In a large bowl, sift together first 5 ingredients and set aside. In a large bowl, beat eggs until light and lemon colored. Gradually beat in sugar and continue beating until volume has at least doubled in size. Gradually fold in flour mixture and lemon rind. Stir in ¾ cup melted butter.

Preheat oven to 350° F. Brush madeleine pan with additional melted butter. Spoon 1 tablespoon batter into each shell, filling it ⅔ full.

Bake 12 minutes or until a toothpick inserted in center comes out clean. Remove cakes from pan to wire rack to cool. Sprinkle with powdered sugar. Wash and butter pan and repeat with remaining dough. Makes 3 dozen madeleines.

German Lebkuchen

Dorothea Schmidt of Regensburg, Germany

3 cups all-purpose flour
1¼ teaspoons ground nutmeg
½ teaspoon ground cloves
1¼ teaspoons ground cinnamon
½ teaspoon ground allspice

½ teaspoon baking soda
1 egg
¾ cup packed brown sugar
½ cup honey
½ cup dark molasses

½ cup chopped citron
½ cup slivered almonds
4 teaspoons water
1 cup powdered sugar

Preheat oven to 375° F. In a large bowl, sift together flour, spices, and baking soda. Set aside.

In a large bowl, beat egg. Add brown sugar and beat until fluffy. Stir in honey and molasses. Gradually stir in flour mixture. Mix well. Stir in citron and almonds.

Lightly grease and flour two 9-by-9-inch baking pans. Spread dough into pans. Bake 12 to 14 minutes.

In a small bowl, combine water and powdered sugar to make glaze. Brush glaze over top of hot lebkuchen. Cool in pans. Cut into bars. Makes 28 bars.

Mexican Sesame-Anise Cookies

Kellye Hammond of West Palm Beach, Florida

2 tablespoons water
1 tablespoon anise seed
⅔ cup granulated sugar

¾ cup butter, softened
⅛ teaspoon baking soda
2 eggs, divided

2 cups sifted all-purpose
flour
⅓ cup sesame seed

In a small saucepan, bring water to a boil. Add anise seed. Remove from heat to steep. In a large bowl, combine sugar, butter, and baking soda. Beat in 1 egg. Set aside. Strain anise-seed liquid into a small bowl and discard seeds. Add strained anise liquid to sugar mixture. Gradually stir in flour and mix well. Cover and chill dough in refrigerator overnight.

Preheat oven to 350° F. Sprinkle sesame seeds in a shallow baking pan. Bake 20 to 22 minutes, stirring 2 or 3 times to toast uniformly. Set aside.

Preheat oven to 400° F. Shape dough into ½-inch balls. Place 3 inches apart on ungreased cookie sheets. Cover cookies with a piece of waxed paper. Using the bottom of a glass, flatten each cookie to a ⅛-inch thickness. Remove waxed paper. In a small bowl, lightly beat remaining egg. Brush egg over tops of cookies. Sprinkle with toasted sesame seeds. Bake 7 to 8 minutes or until lightly browned. Makes 6 dozen cookies.

Buon Natale

Feliz Navidad

OUR HERITAGE

I HEARD THE BELLS ON CHRISTMAS DAY

Henry Wadsworth Longfellow

I heard the bells on Christmas Day
Their old familiar carols play,
    And wild and sweet
    The words repeat
Of 'Peace on earth, good will to men!'

And thought how, as the day had come,
The belfries of all Christendom
    Had rolled along
    The unbroken song
Of 'Peace on earth, good will to men!'

Till ringing, singing on its way,
The world revolved from night to day—
    A voice, a chime,
    A chant sublime
Of 'Peace on earth, good will to men!'

It was as if an earthquake rent
The hearth-stones of a continent,
    And made forlorn
    The households born
Of peace on earth, good will to men!

And in despair I bowed my head;
'There is no peace on earth,' I said.
    'For hate is strong
    And mocks the song
Of peace on earth, good will to men!'

Then pealed the bells more loud and deep;
'God is not dead; nor doth he sleep!
    The wrong shall fail,
    The right prevail,
With peace on earth, good will to men!'

ABOUT THE TEXT

In 1861, American poet Henry Wadsworth Longfellow was facing the Christmas season with a heavy heart following the death of his wife and the outbreak of the American Civil War. As the Christmas bells pealed, their persistent and uplifting message inspired Longfellow to write a poem of his renewed faith. In the 1870s, his words were set to music by English organist John Baptist Caulkin, and the result has since become one of the American people's most beloved carols.

The sound of church bells is heard throughout a snow-covered village in THE VILLAGE CHURCH IN THE SNOW *by artist Charles Leaver (1860–1884). Image from Fine Art Photographic Library Ltd./Private Collection.*

Christmas at Melrose

Leslie Pinckney Hill

Come home with me a little space
And browse about our ancient place,
Lay by your wonted troubles here
And have a turn of Christmas cheer.

These sober walls of weathered stone
Can tell a romance of their own,
And these wide rooms of devious line
Are kindly meant in their design.

Sometimes the north wind
    searches through,
But he shall not be rude to you.
We'll light a log of generous girth
For winter comfort, and the mirth

Of healthy children you shall see
About a sparkling Christmas tree:
Eleanor, leader of the fold;
Hermione with heart of gold;

Elaine with comprehending eyes,
And two more yet of coddling size;
Natalie pondering all that's said,
And Mary with the cherub head—

All these shall give you sweet content
And care-destroying merriment,
While one with true madonna grace
Moves round the glowing fireplace

Where Father loves to muse aside
And Grandma sits in silent pride
And you may chafe the wasting oak,
Or freely pass the kindly joke

To mix with nuts and homemade cake
And apples set on coals to bake.
Or some fine carol we will sing
In honor of the Manger-King,

Or hear great Milton's organ verse
Or Plato's dialogue rehearse
What Socrates with his last breath
Sublimely said of life and death.

These dear delights we fain would share
With friend and kinsman everywhere,
And from our door see them depart,
Each with a little lighter heart.

A festive living room awaits the family in this photo by S. Barth/H. Armstrong Roberts.

THE SECRET OF THE CHRISTMAS TREE

Marjorie Holmes

There is no more beautiful celebration of Christmas than in that great city which belongs to all of us, Washington, D.C. We have toured the White House decked out in all its festive attire; and we have always stood longest in the foyer where, usually, there stands an old-fashioned, ceiling-high, popcorn- and cookie-trimmed Christmas tree. And this, it seems to me, is significant. That in a land of sophistication and plenty, the truest symbol of Christmas is, after all, an old-fashioned family kind of tree.

It brings back all the Christmases past that I knew as a little girl. The fantasy of Santa Claus seemed not in the least at odds with the mail-order catalogs, over which we crouched, making long lists which must be whittled down to plausible proportions. Nor with the hum of Mother's sewing machine at night. Over and over we'd ask, "What for?" If only to hear the beloved reply: "What fur? Cat fur to make kitten britches!" Pressed, she might admit that she was helping Santa's elves. "He's not going to be able to do as much as he'd like to this year." Then among the few new toys of Christmas morning we would find bean bags, doll clothes, little cloth purses for Sunday school.

Mother exchanged gifts with a number of chums who lived elsewhere. She worked openly on their presents, tatting or crocheting doilies and edgings, her shuttle dipping like a little fat bird, the dainty beak of her crochet hook plucking and pulling and picking—almost tasting the threads. She wrapped her efforts in white tissue paper, thin as new snow, and bound them with silver cords. And those rectangles of white and silver seemed in their loveliness to be jeweled blocks for the palace of the Ice Princess.

By now she would have brought forth the family decorations—rough ropes of red and green to loop above the lace curtains and garland the living room. And several paper bells, which lay flat until unfolded, when lo! they bloomed fat and full to hang in doorways and dance in the heat of the hardcoal stove. For us, as for most people, this was all. And although the churches boasted Christmas trees, they were almost unknown in private homes when I was very small.

I shall never forget our first one. Two gentle maiden ladies who lived next door called Mother over one day; and when she returned she was excitedly bearing an enormous box. Desperate for its secret, we plagued her until she yielded at least initials: C.T.D. We spent almost as much time trying to guess their meaning as learning our pieces for the Christmas Eve program at church.

This program, at first mostly songs and recitations, later a pageant, was as much a part of Christmas as hanging up your stocking. We practiced religiously, and if possible got a new dress. Snow squeaked underfoot and sparkled under the streetlights as the family walked to the church. The church was warm and spicy with the scent of the tall fir tree beside the stage.

Sunday school teachers frantically began assembling angels in their proper rows. Shadows moved behind white sheets hung up for curtains. Garbed in bathrobes and turbaned in towels, your father and other men became strangers saying, "Let us go now even unto Bethlehem and see this thing which has come to pass." And the click and swish of the sheets being pulled—and at last the revelation: For there stood Joseph beside a manger with real straw! And Mary cradling a baby—sometimes a big doll, but once a real baby! The minister's new baby! You could hear it crowing and glimpse a flailing hand. It lived! And for a breathless, rapturous moment the living, breathing Christ Child was right there in your midst. . . .

"Good night, Merry Christmas, come to see us!" voices called as families set off along the cold sparkling streets. The snow had usually stopped by

A brother and sister stand in awe of the dazzling ornaments before them. Image from H. Armstrong Roberts.

now. The night was still and clear. All the stars glittered. But there was always one bigger and brighter than the rest. A great gem that seemed to stand still as if to mark the mystery. And you gazed at it in wonder all the way home.

There you scurried for bed and lay hugging yourself, listening to the sweet lullaby of Christmas Eve—parental voices murmuring, the rattle of paper, the tinkle and squeak of treasures unguessed.

Awake before daylight, we found Mother already in the room to restrain us. "Wait!" she said. Something strange was going on. Then when a voice called, "Ready, Rose," she led us forth—into fairyland. Or so it seemed. For there in the living room bloomed a miracle: a Christmas tree! Its candles twinkled and fluttered as if hosts of butterflies and birds had alighted on its branches. From its arms

gleamed dozens of fragile beads and baubles. We stared at it, eyes shining, too dazzled to speak.

And now we knew the secret of the box, C.T.D. "Christmas Tree Decorations," Mother laughed. "The Misses Spicer had them as young ladies in Europe and want our family to have them now."

This lovely gift became the basis for all the trees that followed. We augmented it with strings of popcorn, paper chains, gilded walnuts, and later, when they were plentiful, cranberries. The exquisite fragrance of the tallow candles was replaced by electric bulbs, while tinsel and icicles and fine new ornaments almost crowded out those exquisite early ones. But no tree, however splendid, will be as beautiful as that first one. And no gifts, however expensive or plentiful, can surpass the joy of those precious few we found under it that day.

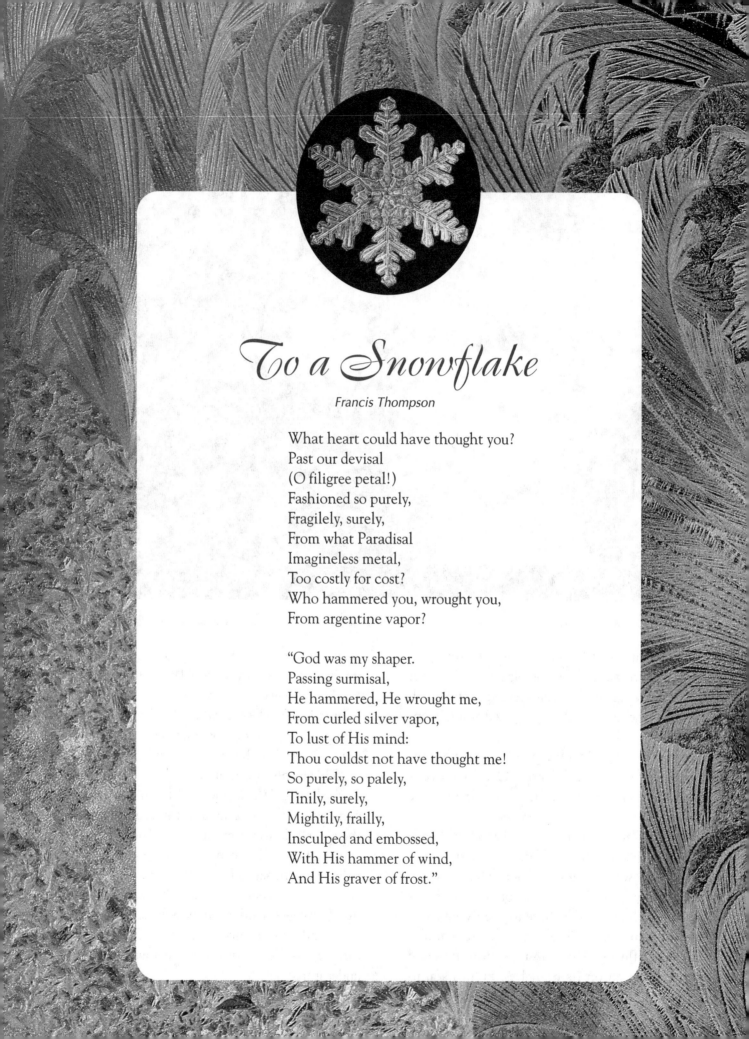

To a Snowflake

Francis Thompson

What heart could have thought you?
Past our devisal
(O filigree petal!)
Fashioned so purely,
Fragilely, surely,
From what Paradisal
Imagineless metal,
Too costly for cost?
Who hammered you, wrought you,
From argentine vapor?

"God was my shaper.
Passing surmisal,
He hammered, He wrought me,
From curled silver vapor,
To lust of His mind:
Thou couldst not have thought me!
So purely, so palely,
Tinily, surely,
Mightily, frailly,
Insculped and embossed,
With His hammer of wind,
And His graver of frost."

Frostwork

Thomas Bailey Aldrich

These winter nights, against my window pane
Nature with busy pencil draws designs
Of ferns and blossoms and fine spray of pines,
Oak-leaf and acorn and fantastic vines,
Which she will make when summer comes again—
Quaint arabesques in argent, flat and cold,
Like curious Chinese etchings. By and by,
I in my leafy garden as of old,
These frosty fantasies shall charm my eye
In azure, damask, emerald, and gold.

Perfection

Marcella Siegel

I have seen the filigreed precision
Of a snowflake, its rays of division
Tracing a star as small as a minute.
I have held in my hand a snow star
Spun from the infinite
And looked at heaven within it.

*Inset: The intricacies of a snowflake are captured by photographer Floyd Dean/FPG International.
Border: This window pane has perhaps never held a view as stunning as these feathers of frost in
Bristol, New Hampshire. Photograph by Johnson's Photography.*

May These Be Yours

Kathryn D. Myers

May these be yours this joyous Christmas season—
Such hope as shepherds harbored long ago,
Such gratitude as wise men felt within them
That prompted each his present to bestow,
Such knowledge as the humble mother pondered,
That He will come to all who will accept,
Such peace as knew the beasts within the stable
Who mid the town's confusion calmly slept,
Such joy as filled the mighty angel chorus
Whose anthems through the star-pierced heavens rang.
May these be yours this joyous Christmas season,
And your heart sing the song the angels sang!

My Christmas Wish

Georgia B. Adams

What do I wish you this Christmas?
Above all, I wish you peace,
A peace of heart and soul and mind
That will with each day increase.

I wish you a calmness of purpose,
A steady and sure resolve
That brings a quiet ambition
Around which all things revolve.

I wish you a tranquil spirit,
Dependence on God above,
A warmness only exceeded
By deep, abiding love.

I wish you a still composure,
Serenity unsurpassed,
I wish harmonious friendships—
The kind that really last.

There may be some storms confronting,
But with this gift of mine
Your Christmas and the days after
Will be peaceful by design.

A festive desktop awaits a holiday letter to a friend. Photo by Nancy Matthews.

WINTER PEACE

Beverly J. Anderson

The snowflakes softly drifted down
And blanketed each country town.
We view a wonderland of white
Beneath the moon of silvery light.

In ermine glory stands each tree
Decked out in lacy filigree.
Each bush and shrub are lovely too
In capes of white with pearly dew.

The rooftops all don crowns of snow,
But inside there's a cheery glow.
The fireplace is warm and bright,
And folks are cozy; hearts are light.

The beauty of this winter night
Is like a fairyland delight;
The streams and brooklets crystal glow,
The moonlight on the pure white snow.

The landscape's robed in silver-white,
So picturesque this starry night.
We view God's winter portrait grand
As peace descends upon the land.

*A gazebo in New London, New Hampshire, is
set aglow by both moonlight and tree lights.
Photo by Johnson's Photography.*

NIGHT OF WONDER

Jean Herrick Warner

Softly, so softly the snowflakes are falling.
Deeply they bury all sounds of the night.
Shimmering in moonlight, the world is now sleeping.
Earth is transformed under down of pure white.

Here in the quiet, time now is suspended,
Matter transcended to silvery light.
Stillness reduces all life to pure being,
Silently, silently buried in white.

Then through the stillness the strains of a carol,
Lilting and pure as a ray of white light,
Break through the silence with voices etheric,
Filling the quiet with "O Holy Night."

SNOW BEAUTY

Mildred L. Jarrell

Oh, what a wondrous sight I see
As snowflakes dress the barren trees.
A world of white and crystal shines,
And ermine edges trim the pines.

How beautiful the meadow lies
As snow falls from the leaden skies
And weaves a blanket warm and white
To cover mother earth at night.

Oh, what a fairyland is this,
The beauty of deep winter's kiss,
The quiet drift and feather flight
Of snowflakes falling in the night.

A SLICE OF LIFE

Edgar A. Guest

A PRAYER FOR THE NEW YEAR

Grant me the strength from day to day
To bear what burdens come my way.
Grant me throughout this bright New Year
More to endure and less to fear.
Help me to live that I may be
From spite and petty malice free.

Let me not bitterly complain
When cherished hopes of mine prove vain,
Or spoil with deeds of hate and rage
Some fair tomorrow's spotless page.
Lord, as the days shall come and go
In courage let me stronger grow.

Let me with patience stand and wait,
A friend to all who find my gate,
Keep me from envy and from scorn;
As shines the sun with every morn
On great and low, so let me give
My love to all who round me live.

Lord, as the New Year dawns today
Help me to put my faults away.
Let me be big in little things;
Grant me the joy which friendship brings.
Keep me from selfishness and spite;
Let me be wise in what is right.

A happy New Year! Grant that I
May bring no tear to any eye.
When this New Year in time shall end
Let it be said I've played the friend,
Have lived and loved and labored here,
And made of it a happy year.

Edgar A. Guest began his illustrious career in 1895 at the age of fourteen, when his work first appeared in the Detroit Free Press. *His column was syndicated in more than three hundred newspapers, and he became known as "The Poet of the People."*

Readers' Forum

Snapshots from Our Ideals Readers

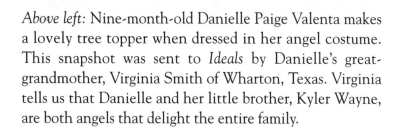

Above left: Nine-month-old Danielle Paige Valenta makes a lovely tree topper when dressed in her angel costume. This snapshot was sent to *Ideals* by Danielle's great-grandmother, Virginia Smith of Wharton, Texas. Virginia tells us that Danielle and her little brother, Kyler Wayne, are both angels that delight the entire family.

Above right: Caleb Crowder, age nine months, and his cousin Ivy Warren, age five months, don matching suits in this photo from great-grandmother Florence Eby of Elkhart, Indiana. According to Florence, it looks as if Ivy is giving Caleb some last minute instructions, perhaps reminding him they need their hats too.

Left: Seven-month-old Mason Jacobusse seems a bit unsure of the duties that come with his costume this Christmas. Mason's picture was sent to us by his great-grandmother, Iva J. Stassen of Holland, Michigan, who tells us she has enjoyed *Ideals* for more than a decade.

Above: Garrett Johnston, age four, and sister Britney, age two, pose for a holiday photo in front of an animated nativity scene. The children visited the site with their grandmother, Judith Perry of Chesapeake, Virginia. Judith tells us that Garrett and Britney were so fascinated by the scene, especially by Baby Jesus, that it took some coaxing to get them to turn around long enough to pose.

Above right: Margaret Saunders of Charlotte, North Carolina, cannot say enough about granddaughter Shanel Nicole Williams, pictured here bundled up for winter in her grandmother's jacket. Margaret tells us that Nikki, as she is called at home, is quite talented and sang a solo during her induction into the National Beta Honor Society.

THANK YOU Virginia Smith, Florence Eby, Iva J. Stassen, Judith Perry, Margaret Saunders, Mrs. Lorene Clark, and Lorraine Dixon for sharing your family photographs with *Ideals.* We hope to hear from other readers who would like to share snapshots with the *Ideals* family. Please include a self-addressed, stamped envelope if you would like the photos returned. Keep your original photographs for safekeeping and send duplicate photos along with your name, address, and telephone number to:

Readers' Forum
Ideals Publications
535 Metroplex Drive, Suite 250
Nashville, Tennessee 37211

ideals

Publisher, Patricia A. Pingry
Editor, Michelle Prater Burke
Designer, Travis Rader
Copy Editor, Elizabeth Kea
Editorial Assistant, Amy Johnson
Contributing Editors, Lansing Christman,
Deana Deck, Pamela Kennedy, and
Nancy Skarmeas

ACKNOWLEDGMENTS

CROWELL, GRACE NOLL. "A Sunny Room in Winter" from *Apples of Gold.* Copyright © 1950 by Grace Noll Crowell. Published by arrangement with HarperCollins Publishers, Inc. All rights reserved. FRENCH, AVIS TURNER. "Winter" from *New Hampshire Troubadour.* Used by permission of the estate of Avis Turner French. FROST, ROBERT. "A Winter Eden" from *The Poetry of Robert Frost,* edited by Edward Connery Lathem. Copyright 1928, © 1969 by Henry Holt and Company, © 1956 by Robert Frost. Reprinted by permission of Henry Holt and Company, LLC. GUEST, EDGAR A. "Prayer for the New Year" from *The Light of Faith.* Used by permission of the estate of Edgar A. Guest. HOLMES, MARJORIE. An excerpt from "The Secret of the Christmas Tree" from *You and I and Yesterday.* Used by permission of the author. L'ENGLE, MADELEINE. "O Simplicitas" from *The Weather of the Heart,* copyright © 1978. Used by permission of Harold Shaw Publishers of WaterBrook Press, Colorado Springs, Colorado. RICHARDSON, ISLA PASCHAL. "Winter Vacancies" from *Wind Among the Pines* by Isla Paschal Richardson. Reprinted by permission of Branden Publishing Company. STRONG, PATIENCE. "Winter Sunshine" from *The Quiet Hour,* copyright © 1939. Reprinted by permission of Rupert Crew Limited. VAN DYKE, HENRY. An excerpt from "To the Child Jesus" from *The Poems of Henry van Dyke* (New York: Charles Scribner's Sons, 1920). Reprinted with the permission of Scribner, a Division of Simon & Schuster. Our sincere thanks to the following authors whom we were unable to locate: Herbert Asquith for "Skating"; Rosaline Guingrich for "Home for Christmas" from *Homespun;* Sudie Stuart Hager for "Transformation" and "Winter Garden" from *Earthbound;* Frances Minturn Howard for "Christmas"; and Helen Welshimer for "Christmas Eve."

Above: Mrs. Lorene Clark of Bremen, Indiana, shares this snapshot of Jacob, her great-grandson. There was no doubt that little Jacob was enjoying all the festivities surrounding his first holiday celebration, especially his new hat.

Right: Jack Parnell III is happy to entertain the family with a few Christmas carols on his great grandmother's piano. Lorraine Dixon of North Bay, Ontario, sent us this picture of Jack, who is one and a half years old. Lorraine tells us she purchased the piano in 1936 with a portion of her seven-dollar-a-week salary. It is now a treasured family heirloom that can be enjoyed by several generations, even Jack!